온라인으로 학습하는 풍부한 실전 어법 문항

Mobile & PC 동시 학습이 가능한

 쎄듀런 온라인 문법 트레이닝 서비스

학생용

❶ 주관식 1

❷ 주관식 2

❸ 주관식 3

❹ 객관식

❺ 선택&주관식

어법끝 ESSENTIAL 온라인 학습 50% 할인 쿠폰

할인 쿠폰 번호 **LFLQWY3M9ZN8**
쿠폰 사용기간 **쿠폰 등록일로부터 90일**

PC 쿠폰 등록 방법

1 쎄듀런에 학생 아이디로 회원가입 후 로그인해 주세요.
2 [결제내역→쿠폰내역]에서 쿠폰 번호를 등록하여 주세요.
3 쿠폰 등록 후 홈페이지 최상단의 [상품소개→(학생전용) 쎄듀캠퍼스]에서
  할인쿠폰을 적용하여 상품을 결제해주세요.
4 [마이캠퍼스→쎄듀캠퍼스→어법끝 ESSENTIAL 클래스]에서 학습을
  시작해주세요.

유의사항
- 본 할인쿠폰과 이용권은 학생 아이디로만 사용 가능합니다.
- 쎄듀캠퍼스 상품은 PC에서만 결제할 수 있습니다.
- 해당 서비스는 내부 사정으로 인해 조기 종료되거나 내용이 변경될 수 있습니다.

어법끝 ESSENTIAL 맛보기 클래스 무료 체험권 (Testing Point 5개)

무료 체험권 번호 **TGVTHMHZGQKB**
클래스 이용기간 **체험권 등록일로부터 30일**

Mobile 쿠폰 등록 방법

1 쎄듀런 앱을 다운로드해 주세요.
2 쎄듀런에 학생 아이디로 회원가입 후 로그인해 주세요.
3 마이캠퍼스에서 [쿠폰등록]을 클릭하여 번호를 입력해주세요.
4 쿠폰 등록 후 [마이캠퍼스→쎄듀캠퍼스→어법끝 ESSENTIAL맛보기
  클래스]에서 학습을 바로 시작해주세요.

PC 쿠폰 등록 방법

1 쎄듀런에 학생 아이디로 회원가입해 주세요.
2 [결제내역→쿠폰내역]에서 쿠폰 번호를 등록하여 주세요.
3 쿠폰 등록 후 [마이캠퍼스→쎄듀캠퍼스→어법끝 ESSENTIAL 맛보기
  클래스]에서 학습을 바로 시작해주세요.

쎄듀런 모바일앱 설치

쎄듀런 홈페이지
www.cedulearn.com

쎄듀런 카페
cafe.naver.com/cedulearnteacher

어법끝
ESSENTIAL

Grammar & Usage

저자

김기훈 現 ㈜쎄듀 대표이사
現 메가스터디 영어영역 대표강사
前 서울특별시 교육청 외국어 교육정책자문위원회 위원
저서 천일문 / 천일문 Training Book / 천일문 GRAMMAR
첫단추 BASIC / Grammar Q / ALL씀 서술형 / Reading Relay
어휘끝 / 어법끝 / 쎄듀 본영어 / 절대평가 PLAN A
The 리딩플레이어 / 빈칸백서 / 오답백서
첫단추 / 파워업 / 쎈쓰업 / 수능영어 절대유형 / 수능실감 등

쎄듀 영어교육연구센터
쎄듀 영어교육센터는 영어 콘텐츠에 대한 전문지식과 경험을 바탕으로
최고의 교육 콘텐츠를 만들고자 최선의 노력을 다하는 전문가 집단입니다.
오혜정 수석연구원 · **구민지** 전임연구원

검토에 도움을 주신 분 | **이홍복** 선생님
원고에 도움을 주신 분 | **한정은**

마케팅 콘텐츠 마케팅 사업본부
제작 정승호
영업 문병구
인디자인 편집 올댓에디팅
디자인 쎄듀 디자인팀
영문교열 Eric Scheusner · Janna Christie

펴낸이 김기훈 | 김진희
펴낸곳 (주)쎄듀 | 서울특별시 강남구 논현로 305 (역삼동)
발행일 2020년 10월 12일 1쇄
내용문의 www.cedubook.com
구입문의 콘텐츠 마케팅 사업본부
Tel. 02-6241-2007
Fax. 02-2058-0209
등록번호 제 22-2472호
ISBN 978-89-6806-206-3

Preface

이 책은 2003년 이후 꾸준히 온·오프라인 대형 서점의 수능 문법서 부문 베스트셀러를 차지하고 있는 어법끝의 최신 개정판으로서 개정률은 40%에 달합니다.

기존의 장점은 적극 살리고 새롭게 반영해야 할 사항들은 모두 고려한 어법끝 ESSENTIAL의 특징은 아래와 같습니다.

첫째, 기출 30년간의 출제 빈도와 최근 8년간의 출제 빈도를 반영하였습니다.

어법 문제는 새로운 포인트가 등장하기보다 계속 출제되던 사항들이 되풀이되는 경향을 보이므로, 기출 사항들이 무엇인지를 아는 것이 가장 중요합니다. 지금까지 실시된 30년간의 대수능, 교육과정평가원과 각 시·도 교육청 주관의 모의평가, 사관학교 및 경찰대 입시에 이르기까지 모든 대입 기출 문제를 종합 분석하여 빈도를 산출하고 이를 반영하였고, 최근 8년간의 출제 빈도가 특히 높은 포인트를 강화하였습니다.

둘째, 함정을 포함하는, 진화하는 어법 문제의 해결 포인트를 반영하였습니다.

진화하는 어법 문제의 흐름을 완벽히 분석하고, 그 해결에 필요한 사항을 모았습니다. 출제진들이 이용하는 함정이 반영된 것들과, 구조 및 독해를 결합한 양질의 많은 어법 문제들을 접할 수 있습니다.

셋째, 내신 서술형 어법 유형을 위한 문제 개수를 대폭 늘렸습니다.

기존 교재에서 본문 설명 부분에 예문으로만 제공되던 것들을 대부분 문제화하였고 네모 어법 중심에서 벗어나 밑줄 어법과 서술형 문제를 포함하는 데에도 적지 않은 노력을 기울였습니다. 서술형에 익숙해지면 내신에 직접적으로 도움이 될 뿐만 아니라, 중요한 포인트들을 좀 더 오래 확실히 기억할 수 있게 해줄 것입니다.

수능 어법 문제는 이제 정형화된 틀이 있고 출제 포인트도 큰 변화 없이 안정이 되어가고 있어서 조금만 노력하면 100% 맞출 수 있는 부분입니다. 이러한 점들을 명심하여 한 문제, 한 포인트도 소홀히 하지 않도록 최선을 다하였습니다. 이렇게 개정된 어법끝 ESSENTIAL이 여러분의 목표 달성에 없어서는 안 될 소중한 한 권으로 기억되기를 진심으로 기원합니다.

어법끝 ESSENTIAL의 구성과 특징

❶ 역대 모든 수능, 모평, 학평 기출문제를
34개의 핵심 어법 포인트로 정리!

❷ 기출 빈도 정보 이원화!
전체 기출 빈도, 최근 기출 빈도

❸ 출제의도와 해결전략
한눈에 보기!

❹ 해결전략의 원리와 과정 이해!

❺ 다양한 문제로 해결전략
적용하기!

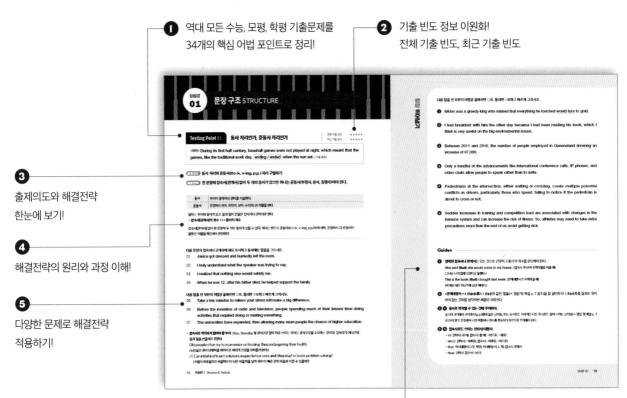

❻ 출제진의 함정 뛰어넘기! 핵심 어법 포인트와 함께
꼭 알아두어야 할 함정 요소들과 해결책 알아보기

❼ 입시 단골 소재의
내용 완결성을
갖춘 문장으로 완벽하게
적용해보기!

도전 고난도 문제

함정 함정 요소 적용 문제

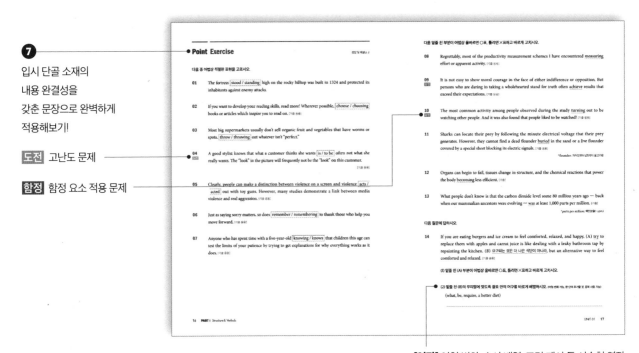

[영작] 어형 변화, 순서 배열, 조건 제시 등 서술형 영작

4

❽ Further Study, LEARN MORE

어법 포인트 중에서 주로 내신에 출제되거나 심화 및 정리 학습이 필요한 중요한 내용을 일목요연 하게 정리하고 문제도 함께 풀이 하는 코너

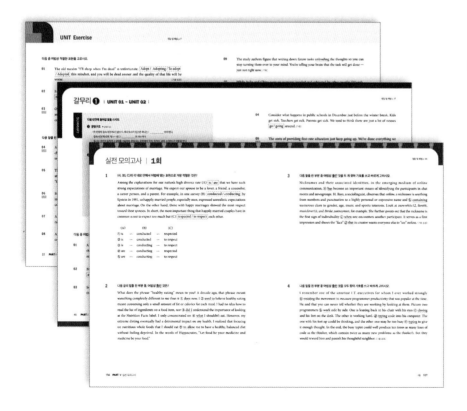

❾ 각종 누적 테스트로 실전 적용력 강화!

· UNIT Exercise

· 갈무리

· PART V: 실전 어법 문제로 구성된 갈무리 모의고사

Contents

기출 30개년 어법 포인트의 **출제 빈도와 시사점**

<30년간 수능, 전국연합, 모의평가 어법 정답 포인트 출제 횟수>

*( )안의 숫자는 오답 포인트 출제 횟수

순위	기출 어법 포인트	출제 횟수				Testing Point
		1994~2023		2016~2023		
1	정동사 vs. 준동사	107	★★★★★	35(13)	★★★★★	01
2	관계대명사와 관계부사	96	★★★★★	19(41)	★★★★★	08, 09
3	능동의 v-ing vs. 수동의 p.p.	69	★★★★★	9(60)	★★★★☆	03
4	that[which] vs. what	68	★★★★★	17(75)	★★★★★	10
5	병렬구조	64	★★★★★	7(27)	★★★★☆	02
6	수식받는 주어의 수일치	53	★★★★★	14(33)	★★★★★	22
7	형용사 자리 vs. 부사 자리	50	★★★★★	9(61)	★★★★☆	12
8	능동태 vs. 수동태	50	★★★★★	7(8)	★★★★☆	27
9	대명사의 성, 수, 격 일치	44	★★★★★	6(61)	★★★★☆	16
10	목적격보어(준동사)	30	★★★★☆	1(21)	★★☆☆☆	19
11	준동사의 동사적 성질	23	★★★★☆	1(7)	★★★☆☆	04
12	전치사 + 명사 vs. 접속사 + SV	22	★★★★☆	0(4)	★★☆☆☆	11
13	감정 변화 동사의 v-ing vs. p.p.	16	★★★★☆	3(2)	★★★☆☆	06
14	구나 절 주어의 수일치	13	★★★★☆	5(5)	★★★☆☆	26
15	동사의 목적어 to-v vs. v-ing	13	★★★★☆	0(5)	★★☆☆☆	05
16	혼동하기 쉬운 형용사와 부사	13	★★★★☆	0(3)	★★☆☆☆	13
17	do의 여러 쓰임(대동사, 동사 강조)	12	★★★☆☆	6(14)	★★★☆☆	20
18	가산, 불가산 명사 구별	10	★★★☆☆	0(1)	★☆☆☆☆	17
19	부분 표현의 수일치	8	★★☆☆☆	1(8)	★★☆☆☆	24
20	현재완료(계속)	7	★★☆☆☆	0(1)	★☆☆☆☆	29
21	간접의문문과 감탄문의 어순	7	★★☆☆☆	0	★☆☆☆☆	10 (Further Study)
22	each, every(+단수) vs. both(+복수)	7	★★☆☆☆	0	★☆☆☆☆	25
23	도치구문의 수일치	6	★★☆☆☆	0(6)	★★☆☆☆	23
24	조동사	6	★★☆☆☆	0	★☆☆☆☆	34
25	비교급을 수식하는 부사	6	★★☆☆☆	0(7)	★★☆☆☆	15
26	비교구문의 형태와 의미	6	★★☆☆☆	1(1)	★★☆☆☆	14
27	used to vs. be used to	5	★★☆☆☆	1(4)	★★☆☆☆	28
28	전치사 to vs. to부정사 to	5	★★☆☆☆	0(6)	★★☆☆☆	07
29	혼동하기 쉬운 동사	5	★★☆☆☆	0(1)	★☆☆☆☆	21
30	혼동하기 쉬운 대명사	5	★★☆☆☆	0(1)	★☆☆☆☆	18
31	과거완료	4	★☆☆☆☆	0(1)	★☆☆☆☆	30
32	당위성을 뜻하는 that절의 (should)	4	★☆☆☆☆	0(1)	★★☆☆☆	33
33	if 가정법	3	★☆☆☆☆	0(1)	★★☆☆☆	32
34	Time(시간) vs. Tense(시제)	2	★☆☆☆☆	0(1)	★☆☆☆☆	31

1   왼쪽 페이지 표의 형광펜 부분에서 볼 수 있듯이, 30년간 출제 순위 1위~10위인 항목들은 최근 8년간 정답으로 출제된 횟수가 많으므로 학습이 특히 집중되어야 할 부분들이다. 이는 출제 포인트들이 계속 반복 출제되고 있다는 것으로도 해석된다.
*최근에 정답으로 출제되는 비중이 낮아진 것들은 능동의 v-ing vs. 수동의 p.p.,형용사 자리 vs. 부사 자리 등이다.

2   최근 8년간은 밑줄 어법 출제 비율이 높아지면서, 오답으로 출제된 어법 포인트에 대한 분석도 필요하다. (출제 횟수 2016~2023 에서 ( ) 안의 숫자가 오답으로 출제된 횟수) 특히 아래 포인트들은 정답보다도 오답으로 출제된 비율이 월등히 높아졌다.

순위	기출 어법 포인트	출제 횟수		오답 출제 비율
		1994~2023	2016~2023	
3	능동의 v-ing vs. 수동의 p.p.	69	9(60)	670%
7	형용사 자리 vs. 부사 자리	50	9(61)	680%
9	대명사의 성, 수, 격 일치	44	6(61)	1020%

3   수능에 2회 이상 출제된 정답 포인트 (전국연합, 모의평가 제외)
특히 3회 이상 반복 출제된 정답 포인트들은 필출(必出)어법으로 간주해야 할 것이다.

<30개년 수능 정답 포인트 출제 횟수 - 전국연합, 모의평가 제외>

기출 어법 포인트	수능 출제 횟수(정답 포인트)
정동사 vs. 준동사	10
병렬구조	8
대명사의 성, 수, 격 일치	7
형용사 자리 vs. 부사 자리	6
능동태 vs. 수동태	5
that[which] vs. what	5
준동사의 동사적 성질	4
능동의 v-ing vs. 수동의 p.p.	4
주어-동사의 수일치	3
관계대명사 = 접속사 + 대명사	3
관계부사 = 접속사 + 부사	2
목적격보어(준동사)의 형태와 능수동	2
동사의 목적어 to-v vs. v-ing	2
간접의문문과 감탄문의 어순	2
조동사의 다의적 의미	2
완전한 구조의 명사절을 이끄는 whether	2

* 이 외에 전치사+명사 vs. 접속사+S+V, 혼동하기 쉬운 형용사와 부사, 가산·불가산 명사 구별, 현재시제 vs. 현재완료(계속), 도치구문의 수일치, each/every+단수 vs. both+복수, 비교구문의 두 가지 빈출 포인트, 접속사 뒤의 v-ing vs. p.p., 당위성 있는 that절의 (should+)동사 원형, 대동사 do가 각각 한 번씩 출제되었다.

진화하는 **어법 문제와 시사점**

과거에는 기본적이고 단순한 해결 포인트를 적용해도 풀 수 있는 것들이 대부분이었지만
최근의 어법 문제를 보면 그런 문제들의 수가 많이 줄어들었다.
최근의 어법 문제들은 적용시켜야 할 개념에 대한 확실한 이해가 바탕이 되어야 할 것을 요구하며,
정확한 해석과 복잡한 문장의 구조 분석이 뒷받침되어야 하는 것들이 소위 킬러 문제로 등장하기도 한다.
이에 대한 정확한 인식 없이 단편적 지식을 기계적으로 적용하면 함정에 빠지는 요소들이 포함되는 문제도 늘고 있다.
아래, 정동사 vs. 준동사 구별하기 문제를 통해 어떻게 진화하고 있는지에 대해 알아보도록 하자.

❶ ~ 2010

절에는 주어와 동사가 있고, 절과 절의 연결은 접속사나 관계사로 한다. 접속사[관계사] 없이 한 문장에 두 개의 동사가 있을 수 없으므로 하나는 반드시 준동사((to-)v, v-ing, p.p.)여야 한다는 원칙은 가장 기본적인 해결 포인트이고 이것만 적용하면 되는 문장들이 대부분 출제되었다. 즉 동사의 개수는 <접속사[관계사]의 개수 + 1>의 법칙이 쉽게 적용된다.

1 Also, **making** sure to bring chocolate to room temperature before eating, // **as** frozen bits of chocolate always strike me as rather hard and tasteless. <2008>

분석 접속사 as가 있으므로 동사의 개수는 2개여야 하는데 앞 절에 동사가 보이지 않으므로 making은 make로 고쳐야 한다. 명령문 형태로서 주어는 생략되어 있다.

(또한, 초콜릿을 먹기 전에 반드시 상온에 두도록 해야 하는데, 왜냐하면 냉동된 초콜릿 조각은 항상 내게는 약간 딱딱하고 맛이 없게 느껴지기 때문이다. room temperature 상온 strike A (as ~) A에게 (~하다는) 인상[느낌]을 주다)

2 Don't wash the broccoli before storing it // **since** moisture on its surface | encourages / to encourage | the growth of mold. <2009>

분석 원인을 뜻하는 접속사 since(~이므로)가 있으므로 동사의 개수는 2개여야 하는데 since절에 동사가 보이지 않으므로 encourages를 골라야 한다.

(브로콜리를 저장하기 전에 세척하지 마라(브로콜리는 씻지 않고 저장해라). 왜냐하면 표면의 수분이 곰팡이의 성장을 촉진하기 때문이다. encourage 촉진하다, 장려하다 mold 곰팡이)

❷ 2011 ~ 2014

2011년 이후에도 기본적인 원칙이 적용되는 문제가 출제되긴 했지만, 기본적인 해결 포인트만으로는 해결이 어려울 수 있는 문제들이 등장하기 시작했다. 기본적인 해결 포인트에서 관건이 되는 것이 접속사, 관계사, 동사 유무를 파악하는 것인데 그 파악이 쉽지 않은 문제들이 등장한 것이다. 대표적으로는 접속사나 관계사가 생략된 경우, 동사로 보이지만 사실은 과거분사 후치 수식인 경우, 접속사나 관계사로도 쓰이는 단어지만 사실은 전치사나 대명사 등으로 쓰인 경우 등이다.

(자세한 내용은 ☞ UNIT 01 문장 구조 STRUCTURE Testing Point 01 동사 자리인가, 준동사 자리인가 참조)

3　For most of recorded history, people lived where they were born, did what their parents had done, and associated with those who were doing the same. ...(중략)... This left most folks with little to decide for themselves. But the industrial and technological revolutions changed all that, and the resulting explosion of personal liberty **creating** an array of options, alternatives, and decisions that our ancestors never faced. <2011>

分析　밑줄이 포함된 문장은 접속사 and와 관계대명사 that이 있어 동사가 세 개 필요한데, and가 이끄는 절에 동사가 보이지 않으므로 creating을 과거시제 동사 created로 고쳐야 한다. 접속사 and 바로 앞의 that은 접속사가 아니라 앞 문장의 내용을 받는 대명사임에 주의해야 한다. 등위접속사 and나 or는 대부분 단어나 구를 연결하지만 절과 절을 연결할 수도 있음을 기억해두자. 참고로, 같은 등위접속사인 but이나 so는 절과 절을 연결해서 쓰는 경우가 많아서, 문법적으로 옳지는 않지만 문장 앞에도 많이 쓰인다. 이때는 마치 접속부사처럼 쓰인 것이므로 이를 접속사로 간주해서 동사 개수가 하나 더 많아야 하는 것으로 판단하면 안 된다.

But the industrial and technological revolutions changed all that, and the resulting explosion of personal
　　　　　　　　　　　　　　　　　　S1　　　　　　　V1　　　　　　　　　　　　　　S2
liberty **created** an array of options, alternatives, and decisions [that our ancestors never faced].
　　　　V2　　　　　　　　　　　　　　　　　　　　　　　S'　　　　　V'

(대부분의 기록된 역사에서, 사람들은 태어난 곳에서 살고 그들의 부모가 했던 일을 하고 그리고 같은 일을 하고 있는 사람들과 어울렸다. … 이는 대부분의 사람들에게 스스로 결정할 여지를 거의 남기지 않았다. 그러나 산업과 기술 혁명은 그 모든 것들을 바꾸었고, 결과적으로 초래된 개인의 자유의 폭발은 우리 조상들이 결코 직면하지 않았던 다수의 선택, 대안, 그리고 결정을 만들어 냈다. **an array of** 다수의; 죽 늘어서 있는)

❸ 2015 ~

2014년도까지의 출제 기조가 그대로 유지되면서 아래와 같은 좀 더 복잡하고 까다로운 문장들도 출제되고 있다. 내용적으로 추상성이 높아지면 체감 난이도가 따라서 더 올라간다.

4　As long as he keeps his information to himself, he may feel superior to those who do not know it. But knowing and not telling does not give him that feeling of "superiority that, so to say, latently contained in the secret, fully **actualizing** itself only at the moment of disclosure." This is the main motive for gossiping about well-known figures and superiors. <2020>

*latently: 잠재적으로

分析　밑줄이 포함된 문장에 관계대명사 that이 보이므로 동사는 두 개가 필요한데, contained는 that feeling of superiority를 수식하는 어구를 이끄는 과거분사이므로 밑줄은 동사 자리이다. 주격 관계대명사인 that의 선행사는 단수명사인 that feeling of superiority이고 현재 사실을 말하고 있으므로 actualizes가 되어야 한다.

But knowing and not telling does not give him that feeling of "superiority [that, so to say, (latently
　　　S　　　　　　　　V　　　　IO　　　　　　　DO　　　　　　　S'
contained in the secret,) fully **actualizes** itself only at the moment of disclosure]."
　　　　　　　　　　　　　　　　　V'

(그가 정보를 혼자만 알고 있는 한, 그는 그 정보를 모르는 사람들한테 우월감을 가질지도 모른다. 그러나 알고 있는데 말하지 않는 것은, "말하자면 그 비밀 속에 잠재적으로 들어 있다가 폭로의 순간에만 스스로를 완전히 실현시키는 우월감"을 그에게 주지 않는다. 이것이 잘 알려진 인물들과 우월한 사람들에 대하여 뒷공론을 하는 주된 동기이다. **feel superior to** 우월감을 갖다 **disclosure** 폭로)

PART

I

Structure & Verbals

Testing Point 01 　동사 자리인가, 준동사 자리인가

전체 기출 빈도 　◆◆◆◆◆
최근 기출 빈도 　◆◆◆◆◆

<예제> During its first half century, baseball games were not played at night, which meant that the games, like the traditional work day, | ending / ended | when the sun set. [기출 응용]

출제의도 동사 자리와 준동사((to-)v, v-ing, p.p.) 자리 구별하기

해결전략 한 문장에 접속사[관계사] 없이 두 개의 동사가 있으면 하나는 준동사(부정사, 분사, 동명사)여야 한다.

동사	주어의 동작이나 상태를 서술한다.
준동사	문장에서 주어, 목적어, 보어, 수식어(구) 역할을 한다.

절에는 주어와 동사가 있고, 절과 절의 연결은 접속사나 관계사로 한다.

• 접속사[관계사]의 개수 + 1 = 동사의 개수

접속사[관계사] 없이 한 문장에 두 개의 동사가 있을 수 없다. 하나는 반드시 준동사((to-)v, v-ing, p.p.)여야 하며, 문장에서 각 준동사의 알맞은 역할을 확인하여 판단한다.

다음 문장의 접속사나 관계사에 네모 표시하고 동사에는 밑줄을 그으시오.

01　　Janice got dressed and hurriedly left the room.

02　　I truly understand what the speaker was trying to say.

03　　I realized that nothing else would satisfy me.

04　　When he was 12, after his father died, he helped support the family.

다음 밑줄 친 부분이 어법상 올바르면 ○표, 틀리면 ✕표하고 바르게 고치시오.

05　　Take a few minutes to relieve your stress will make a big difference.

06　　Before the invention of radio and television, people spending much of their leisure time doing activities that required doing or making something.

07　　The universities have expanded, thus allowing many more people the chance of higher education.

• **접속사로 착각하지 말아야 할 부사**: thus, thereby 등 분사구문 앞에 자주 쓰이는 부사는 분사구문을 수식하는 것이다. 접속사가 아니므로 절과 절을 연결하지 못한다.

Old people often try to economize on heating, **thus** *endangering* their health.
(노인들은 흔히 난방비를 아끼려고 하다가 건강을 위태롭게 한다.)

cf. Can initial inefficient solutions inspire better ones **and thus** *lead* to faster problem solving?
(처음의 비효율적인 해결책이 더 나은 해결책을 낳게 하여 더 빠른 문제 해결로 이끌 수 있을까?)

다음 밑줄 친 부분이 어법상 올바르면 ○표, 틀리면 ×표하고 바르게 고치시오.

❶ Midas was a greedy king who wished that everything he touched <u>would turn</u> to gold.

❷ I had breakfast with him the other day because I had been reading his book, which I think <u>is</u> very useful on the big environmental issues.

❸ Between 2011 and 2016, the number of people employed in Queensland <u>showing</u> an increase of 97,099.

❹ Only a handful of the advancements like international conference calls, IP phones, and video chats <u>allow</u> people to speak rather than to write.

❺ Pedestrians at the intersection, either waiting or crossing, create multiple potential conflicts as drivers, particularly those who speed, <u>failing</u> to notice if the pedestrian is about to cross or not.

❻ Sudden increases in training and competition load are associated with changes in the immune system and can increase the risk of illness. So, athletes may need to take extra precautions more than the rest of us <u>avoid</u> getting sick.

Guides

❶ **생략된 접속사나 관계사**는 있는 것으로 간주하고 동사의 개수를 판단해야 한다.
She *said* (**that**) she *would come to* my house. (접속사 that이 목적어절을 이끌 때)
(그녀는 나의 집에 오겠다고 말했다.)
This *is* the book (**that**) I *bought* last week. (관계대명사가 목적격일 때)
(이 책은 내가 지난주에 샀던 책이다.)

❷ **<관계대명사 + I think류>:** I think와 같은 절들(☞ 정답 및 해설 p. 2 참조)을 잘 알아두자. I think류를 괄호로 묶어 마치 없는 것처럼 생각하면 해결이 쉬워진다.

❸❹ **동사로 착각할 수 있는 것에 주의하자.**
동사의 과거형과 과거분사(p.p.)형이 같은 단어들, 또는 동사로도 쓰이지만 다른 품사로도 많이 쓰이는 단어들(☞ 정답 및 해설 p. 3 참조)의 경우, 문장에서 쓰인 역할이나 품사를 혼동하기 쉬우므로 주의해야 한다.

❺❻ **접속사로도 쓰이는 전치사/대명사**
• as: 전치사(~로서), 접속사(~할 때; ~이므로; ~ 대로)
• since: 전치사(~ 이후로), 접속사(~ 이후로; ~이므로)
• that: 지시대명사(그것, 저것), 지시형용사(그, 저), 접속사, 관계사
• than: 전치사, 접속사(~보다)

Point Exercise

정답 및 해설 p. 3

다음 중 어법상 적절한 표현을 고르시오.

01 The fortress ⎡stood / standing⎤ high on the rocky hilltop was built in 1324 and protected its inhabitants against enemy attacks.

02 If you want to develop your reading skills, read more! Wherever possible, ⎡choose / choosing⎤ books or articles which inspire you to read on. [기출 응용]

03 Most big supermarkets usually don't sell organic fruit and vegetables that have worms or spots, ⎡throw / throwing⎤ out whatever isn't "perfect."

04 도전 A good stylist knows that what a customer thinks she wants ⎡is / to be⎤ often not what she really wants. The "look" in the picture will frequently not be the "look" on this customer.

[기출 응용]

05 Clearly, people can make a distinction between violence on a screen and violence ⎡acts / acted⎤ out with toy guns. However, many studies demonstrate a link between media violence and real aggression. [기출 응용]

06 Just as saying sorry matters, so does ⎡remember / remembering⎤ to thank those who help you move forward. [기출 응용]

07 Anyone who has spent time with a five-year-old ⎡knowing / knows⎤ that children this age can test the limits of your patience by trying to get explanations for why everything works as it does. [기출 응용]

다음 밑줄 친 부분이 어법상 올바르면 ○표, 틀리면 ×표하고 바르게 고치시오.

08 Regrettably, most of the productivity measurement schemes I have encountered <u>measuring</u> effort or apparent activity. [기출 응용]

09 함정 It is not easy to show moral courage in the face of either indifference or opposition. But persons who are daring in taking a wholehearted stand for truth often <u>achieve</u> results that exceed their expectations. [기출 응용]

10 함정 The most common activity among people observed during the study <u>turning</u> out to be watching other people. And it was also found that people liked to be watched! [기출 응용]

11 Sharks can locate their prey by following the minute electrical voltage that their prey generates. However, they cannot find a dead flounder <u>buried</u> in the sand or a live flounder covered by a special sheet blocking its electric signals. [기출 응용]

*flounder: 가자밋과와 넙칫과의 물고기류

12 Organs can begin to fail, tissues change in structure, and the chemical reactions that power the body <u>becoming</u> less efficient. [기출]

13 What people don't know is that the carbon dioxide level some 80 million years ago — back when our mammalian ancestors were evolving — <u>was</u> at least 1,000 parts per million. [기출]

*parts per million: 백만분율(= ppm.)

다음 질문에 답하시오.

14 If you are eating burgers and ice cream to feel comforted, relaxed, and happy, (A) <u>try</u> to replace them with apples and carrot juice is like dealing with a leaky bathroom tap by repainting the kitchen. (B) 요구되는 것은 더 나은 식단이 아니라, but an alternative way to feel comforted and relaxed. [기출 응용]

(1) 밑줄 친 (A) 부분이 어법상 올바르면 ○표, 틀리면 ×표하고 바르게 고치시오.

(2) 밑줄 친 (B)의 우리말에 맞도록 괄호 안의 어구를 바르게 배열하시오. (어형 변화 가능, 한 단어 추가할 것, 중복 사용 가능)

(what, be, require, a better diet)

<예제> The exposure to fine art allowed him to have an amazing aesthetic experience and recognize / recognized his calling to be an artist.

출제의도 병렬 관계의 문장 구조 파악하기

해결전략 병렬구조를 이끄는 접속사와 구문을 알아두고, 정확한 문장 해석을 통해 문맥상 올바로 연결되는 것을 찾아야 한다.

A+등위접속사+B	등위접속사 and, but, or 등은 문법적으로 대등한 형태의 A와 B를 연결한다. 네모나 밑줄 앞에 등위접속사가 있을 경우, 병렬구조 문제일 가능성이 매우 높다.

병렬구조 문제에서 네모나 밑줄은 대개 B에 주어지며 앞에서 A를 잘 찾아내야 한다. <A+ ~ +등위접속사+B>의 구조로, A와 등위접속사가 서로 떨어져 있고 '~' 부분에는 혼동을 일으키기 위한 다른 어형들이 포함되는 경우가 많다.

다음 문장의 병렬구조를 파악하여 괄호 안에 주어진 동사를 올바른 형태로 바꾸시오.

01 Stop talking nonsense and (be) ＿＿＿＿＿＿＿ sincere.

02 He quit working for a boss and (set) ＿＿＿＿＿＿＿ out on his own business last year.

03 Jim hit on a new idea of packaging the product and (advertise) ＿＿＿＿＿＿ it online.

04 The partner only has two options. He can take what's offered or (refuse) ＿＿＿＿＿＿ to take anything. [기출 응용]

• 등위접속사는 어구나 절도 연결할 수 있음을 기억하자.
  Figure out <u>where to go</u> and <u>whom to ask</u> to get the information you need.
  ＿＿＿＿A＿＿＿＿ ＿＿＿＿B＿＿＿＿
  (네가 원하는 정보를 얻기 위해 어디로 갈지와 누구에게 물어볼지 파악해라.)

상관접속사	등위접속사를 포함하는 구문의 A, B도 문법적으로 대등한 형태이다.
	• both A **and** B • (n)either A **(n)or** B
	• not only A **but** also B • not A **but** B

다음 밑줄 친 부분과 병렬구조를 이루는 것을 찾아 밑줄 치시오.

05 Technology plays a huge role in our lives both <u>at work</u> and <u>during play</u>.

06 This kind of talk is not only <u>meaningless</u> but also <u>far</u> from the truth.

| 비교, 대조 등 | 비교나 대조 대상이 되는 A, B도 문법적으로 대등한 형태이다.
이 외에도 from A to B, between A and B 등의 연결 구조에서도 A, B는 문법적으로 대등한 형태이다. |

다음 문장의 병렬구조를 파악하여 괄호 안에 주어진 동사를 올바른 형태로 바꾸시오.

07 Using a mobile phone while driving can be more dangerous than (be) _____ drunk behind the wheel.

08 As a leader, you must transition from doing the work yourself to (get) _____ the work done with others.

함정 뛰어넘기

다음 중 어법상 적절한 표현을 고르시오.

❶ Baseball has no set length of time within which the game must be completed. The pace of the game is therefore leisurely and unhurried / unhurriedly . [기출]

❷ A painting restorer's goal is to respect the artist's intent, but at the same time making / to make the painting a visually coherent work of art. [기출 응용]

❸ The authors are well-served by their publisher; the volume is attractive and relative / relatively free of typographical error.

Guides

❶ -ly 형용사(☞ 정답 및 해설 p. 5 참조)의 품사를 착각하지 않도록 주의한다.

❷ A ~ + 등위접속사 + 부사(구) + B
병렬구조 문제에서 등위접속사와 B 사이에 부사(구)가 위치한 경우에 주의한다. 부사(구)의 위치는 문장에서 비교적 자유롭다는 점을 늘 잊지 말아야 한다.

❸ A(형용사) + 등위접속사 + 부사(구) + B(형용사)
네모나 밑줄 바로 앞에 등위접속사가 있어 병렬구조 문제로 보이지만 사실은 부사 자리를 묻는 문제임에 주의한다.

Point Exercise

정답 및 해설 p. 6

다음 중 어법상 적절한 표현을 고르시오.

01   Coming home from work the other day, I saw a woman trying to turn onto the main street and ⌊have / having⌋ very little luck because of the constant stream of traffic. [기출 응용]

02   Albert Einstein remembered seeing a pocket compass when he was five years old and ⌊marveling / marveled⌋ that the needle always pointed north. In that moment, Einstein recalled, he "felt something deeply hidden behind things." [기출 응용]

03   He had university students read a personality description of someone and then ⌊summarize / summarized⌋ it for someone else who was believed either to like or to dislike this person.

[기출 응용]

04   In a subsequent session, each mother was asked to watch the play session that was videotaped earlier and ⌊say / said⌋ aloud what she thought the baby was feeling.

05   Once you have a basic grasp of vocabulary, you should stop thinking in your own language
[도전] and ⌊try / trying⌋ to translate everything, as this slows your progress down and narrows your thinking.

06   He used a bicycle to improve efficiency for his windmill. The windmill was able to generate electricity for his parents' house. His next goal is to supply enough energy for his entire village and eventually ⌊go / goes⌋ to college. [기출 응용]

다음 밑줄 친 부분이 어법상 올바르면 ○표, 틀리면 ×표하고 바르게 고치시오.

07   Robots and astronauts use much of the same equipment in space. But a human is much more capable of operating those instruments accurately and <u>to place</u> them in appropriate and useful positions. [기출 응용]

08   A book review is a personal assessment which explains how well an author has covered a specific topic. As a reviewer, you analyze the book for how it tells a story and <u>evaluates</u> the quality of writing and organization. [기출 응용]

09   Above the television hangs a large photograph of Neil Armstrong standing on the surface of the moon and <u>salutes</u> a stiff American flag. [기출 응용]

10   While many people like to take advantage of their time off by traveling, others prefer to stay at home and work on household projects. They might spend their vacation painting a porch or <u>wash</u> all the windows in their apartment. [기출 응용]

11   The unexpected combination of skilled musicians resulted in a continuous and <u>fairly</u> enthusiastic response from the audience, who loudly clapped at each interruption between songs.

12   Occasionally individuals do not merely come out, as well as clearly state what is troubling them, and instead <u>select</u> a more indirect means of expressing their annoyance. [기출 응용]

우리말에 맞도록 괄호 안의 어구를 바르게 배열하시오. (어형 변화 가능, 주어진 어구로만 배열할 것)

13   새 일자리를 찾는 데는 많은 방법이 있다. 그것들은 인터넷 또는 신문의 광고된 일자리들을 찾는 것에서부터 직접 고용주와 연락하는 것에 이른다.

(range, from, to, contact, search for, on the Internet or in newspapers, advertised positions, employers)

There are many ways to find a new job. They _____

_____ directly.

다음 중 어법상 적절한 표현을 고르시오.

01 The old maxim "I'll sleep when I'm dead" is unfortunate. Adopt / Adopting / To adopt / Adopted this mindset, and you will be dead sooner and the quality of that life will be worse. [기출 응용]

02 It is important that we are aware when one of our cognitive biases is activated and that we make / made a conscious choice to overcome that bias. [기출 응용]

03 도전 One simple explanation to explain why routine enables difficult things to become easy is that as we repeatedly do a certain task the neurons, or nerve cells, make / making / to make new connections through communication gateways called "synapses." [기출 응용]

다음 밑줄 친 부분이 어법상 올바르면 ○표, 틀리면 ✕표하고 바르게 고치시오.

04 도전 Artists usually limit themselves by choice of material and form of expression. To make the choice to express a feeling by carving a specific form from a rock, without the use of high technology or colors, <u>restricting</u> the artist significantly. [기출 응용]

05 The Chinese saw the world as consisting of continuously interacting substances, so their attempts to understand it <u>causing</u> them to be oriented toward the complexities of the entire "field" — that is, the context or environment as a whole. [기출]

06 도전 Beginning in the seventh century A.D., relatively <u>sustained</u> and at times intense intercivilizational contacts developed between Islam and the West and Islam and India. Most commercial, cultural, and military interactions, however, were within civilizations. [기출]

07 An individual neuron <u>sends</u> a signal in the brain uses as much energy as a leg muscle cell running a marathon.

08 Around 10,000 years ago, humans learned to cultivate plants and <u>tame</u> animals and thus control important matter and energy flows. [기출]

09 The study authors figure that writing down future tasks <u>unloading</u> the thoughts so you can stop turning them over in your mind. You're telling your brain that the task will get done — just not right now. [기출]

10 While India and China were on occasion invaded and subjected by other peoples (Moguls, Mongols), both civilizations <u>having</u> extensive times of "warring states" within their own civilization as well. [기출]

11 Suddenly, a phrase I once read <u>came</u> floating into my mind: 'You must do him or her a kindness for inner reasons, not because someone is keeping score or because you will be punished if you don't.' [기출]

12 We can think about ourselves as if we are not part of ourselves. Research on primate behavior indicates that even our closest cousins, the chimpanzees, <u>lacking</u> this ability. [기출]

13 The availability heuristic refers to a common mistake that our brains make by assuming that the instances or examples that come to mind easily <u>are</u> also the most important or prevalent. It shows that we make our decisions based on the recency of events. [기출 응용]

*availability heuristic: 가용성[기억 용이성] 편향

다음 문장에서 어법상 틀린 부분을 찾아 밑줄을 긋고 바르게 고치시오.

14
도전
Most of us are not aware of flaws in our reasoning processes, but professionals who work to convince us of certain viewpoints to study the research on human decision making to determine how to exploit our weaknesses to make us more susceptible to their messages.

[기출 응용]

15 The Birmingham campaign, which was a series of protests against racial segregation in Birmingham, ending with a victory when many segregation signs in Birmingham businesses were removed, and public places became accessible to people of all races.

UNIT 02 준동사 VERBALS

Testing Point 03	**의미상 주어와의 관계가 능동이면 v-ing, 수동이면 p.p.**

전체 기출 빈도 ✦✦✦✦✦
최근 기출 빈도 ✦✦✦✦✧

<예제> Many African language speakers would consider it absurd to use a single word like "cousin" to describe both male and female relatives, or not to distinguish whether the person | described / describing | is related by blood to the speaker's father or to his mother. [기출]

출제의도 분사의 능동, 수동 구분하기

해결전략 의미상 주어와 분사를 주어, 동사의 관계로 놓고 능동, 수동을 판별한다.

분사 + 명사 / 명사 + 분사 ~	의미상 주어 = 분사의 수식을 받는 명사

다음 중 어법상 적절한 표현을 고르시오.

01   Government measures | restricting / restricted | the use of plastic bags are gradually taking root among retailers. [기출 응용]

02   Among the | displaying / displayed | drawings will be works of contemporary artists as well as those of the old masters.

03   The orientation was boring, but not as boring as the meeting | holding / held | afterward.

(접속사 +) 분사구문, S+V ~	분사구문의 의미상 주어 = 문장의 주어

04   Jack crossed the river, | holding / held | tightly the hand of his seven-year-old daughter.

05 | Picking / Picked | either by hand or by machine, the grapes are taken to the winery. [기출 응용]

06   When | exposing / exposed | to the sun, your skin darkens but your hair lightens.

• <분사구문의 의미상 주어≠문장의 주어>인 경우, 분사구문 앞에 의미상 주어를 써준다.

   Today **being** Sunday, **we** are permitted to work a little less hurriedly than usual.
          └─────── ≠ ───────┘

   = As ***today*** **is** Sunday, **we** are permitted ~.
   (오늘은 일요일이라서 우리는 평소보다 일을 좀 덜 서둘러 하는 것이 허용된다.)

with + (대)명사 + 분사 (~이 …한 채로)	(대)명사=의미상 주어

07 With nobody ⏢ watching / watched ⏢ , the band played the song till the end.

08 A fire partially destroyed the church, but it was rebuilt with all its original features ⏢ preserving / preserved ⏢ .

동사 + 목적어 + 목적격보어	목적어=의미상 주어 (☞ Testing Point 19 동사에 따른 목적격보어의 형태에 주의하라! 참조)

09 I saw her ⏢ cooking / cooked ⏢ the dish on TV.

10 We saw the dish ⏢ serving / served ⏢ to other customers.

학정 뛰어넘기

다음 중 어법상 적절한 표현을 고르시오.

❶ At the conference, the children ⏢ attending / attended ⏢ educational sessions, taking field trips to museums and listening to presentations from other children. [기출 응용]

❷ He goes on to describe his daily routine of strolling through the village ⏢ observed / observing ⏢ the lives of other people. [기출 응용]

❸ Hardcopy documents can hamper the process of information flow due to ⏢ missing / missed ⏢ documents or misplaced files.

Guides

❶ **명사를 수식하는 분사 자리 vs. 동사 자리**
특히 동사의 과거형이 p.p.와 같은 형태인 경우, 명사를 수식하는 분사 자리가 확실한지를 판단하기 위해 해당 절의 동사를 반드시 확인하도록 한다. (☞ Testing Point 01 동사 자리인가, 준동사 자리인가 참조)

❷ **명사를 수식하는 분사 vs. 분사구문**
분사구문은 문장 앞, 주어와 동사 사이, 문장 끝에 모두 올 수 있는데, 문장 끝에 올 경우 콤마 없이 오기도 한다. 이때 분사 바로 앞에 명사가 있으면 그 명사를 수식하는 분사로 착각할 수 있다. 반대로, 명사를 수식하는 분사를 분사구문으로 혼동하지도 말아야 한다.

❸ **능동, 수동 관계 구분이 모호하면서 잘 쓰이는 어구들은 숙어처럼 암기하라.**
a **missing** child(실종된 아이) / **opposing** ideas(대립되는 의견) / a **retired** teacher(은퇴한 교사) 등, 대부분 분사 형태가 굳어져서 형용사가 되었거나 관용적으로 쓰이는 것들은 어구로 암기해두는 것이 효율적이다. (☞ 정답 및 해설 p. 10 참조)

Point Exercise

정답 및 해설 p. 10

다음 중 어법상 적절한 표현을 고르시오.

01 Spending / Spent an enormous amount of computing time, the robot finally recognizes this collection of circles, ovals, spirals, straight lines, and curly lines as a table. [기출 응용]

02 Having said positive things about someone, they also then liked the person more themselves. Asked / Asking to recall what they had read, they remembered the description as being more positive than it was. [기출 응용]

03 It was going to be a long day, but Vince regarded himself as a highly experiencing / experienced traveller and claimed never to have suffered jet-lag in his life.

04 It is difficult to determine the shape of fire. There is a simplified design, adopted / adopting for use in posters and signs. It resembles a lotus flower. [기출 응용]

*lotus flower: 연꽃

05 If you move your hand two inches to emphasize a point when speaking / spoken to one person, you may have to move it as much as two feet in front of a large audience. [기출 응용]

06 When installing / installed in a window frame, the glass would be placed with the thicker side down for the sake of stability. [기출 응용]

07 Everyone (A) summoning / summoned to appear for jury duty must be present in the jury room at nine o'clock. A few minutes later, the court clerk shows a movie (B) outlined / outlining what is going to happen later in the day as the jury is selected for a particular trial. [기출 응용]

08
도전
Depressed people have a shortage of GABA, a neurotransmitter (A) linking / linked to a visual skill. This substance helps us ignore details (B) surrounding / surrounded the object our eyes are focused on. [기출 응용]

*neurotransmitter: 신경전달물질

다음 밑줄 친 부분이 어법상 올바르면 ○표, 틀리면 ✕표하고 바르게 고치시오.

09 The arts often teach moral lessons or values <u>considering</u> important in a society and are also used to send political messages or draw attention to social issues. [기출 응용]

10 If you need to suck liquid out of the phone, try using a vacuum cleaner. Eliminate all residual moisture by drawing it away with a vacuum cleaner <u>held</u> over the affected areas for up to twenty minutes. [기출 응용]

11 Hierarchies are good at weeding out obviously bad ideas. By the time an idea makes it all the way up the chain, it will have been compared to all the other ideas in the system, with the obviously good ideas <u>ranked</u> at the top. [기출 응용]

12 When (A) <u>practicing</u> a new piece, (B) <u>advancing</u> musicians have a very (C) <u>detailed</u> mental representation of the music they use to guide their practice and, ultimately, their performance of a piece. [기출 응용]

빈칸에 알맞은 말을 <보기>에서 골라 필요하면 변형하여 쓰시오.

<보기>   form   situate

13 (A) _____ at an elevation of 1,350m, the city of Kathmandu enjoys a warm climate year-round that makes life there pleasant. It lies almost in the center of a basin, (B) _____ a square about 5km north-south and 5km east-west. [기출 응용]

우리말에 맞도록 괄호 안의 어구를 바르게 배열하시오. (어형 변화 가능, 주어진 어구로만 배열할 것)

14 모든 치즈는 다양한 박테리아가 첨가된 우유로 만들어진다. 치즈를 만드는 데 사용되는 박테리아는 사람들에게 해롭지 않다. [기출 응용]

(A) (various, has, to, bacteria, add, it)   (B) (harmful, cheese, be, use, not, to make, to people)

All cheeses are made from milk that (A) _____.
The bacteria (B) _____.

<예제> Jump rope is great for development / developing cooperative skills among children. [기출 응용]

출제의도 준동사의 동사적 성질 이해하기

해결전략 준동사는 동사적 성질이 있으므로 목적어를 취할 수 있고 부사가 수식할 수 있다. 동사처럼 태와 시제를 나타낼 수도 있다. 의미상 주어와의 의미 관계를 살펴 태를 구분하고, 문장의 동사가 나타내는 때와의 전후 관계를 통해 알맞은 시제 형태를 판단한다.

v-ing(동명사) + 목적어	동명사는 동사에서 온 것이므로 목적어를 바로 취할 수 있지만 동명사를 명사로 바꾸면 적절한 전치사가 필요하다. (e.g. knowing the theory vs. knowledge **of** the theory, analyzing the causes vs. analysis **of** the causes)

다음 중 어법상 적절한 표현을 고르시오.

01   To solve the problem, one of the ways is improving / improvement the quality of living conditions.

02   The therapist will help the participants set specific activity goals, the aim of which is improving / improvement of daily living function.

부사로 수식	준동사는 동사에서 나온 것이므로 부사로 수식한다.

03   By careful / carefully considering all the options, she made a wise decision.

04   Strong / Strongly warning about the side effects of the drug, he urged people to boycott it.

to부정사와 동명사의 태	의미상 주어와의 관계가 능동 (to-v / v-ing)
	의미상 주어와의 관계가 수동 (to be p.p. / being p.p.)
	(☞ Testing Point 03 의미상 주어와의 관계가 능동이면 v-ing, 수동이면 p.p. /
	☞ Testing Point 19 동사에 따른 목적격보어의 형태에 주의하라! 참조)

다음 네모 안의 준동사에 대한 의미상 주어에 밑줄을 긋고 어법상 적절한 표현을 고르시오.

05   The books to refund / be refunded are on the table.

06   The child was afraid of leaving / being left alone in the dark.

to have p.p. / having p.p.	문장의 동사보다 앞선 때의 동작이나 상태

다음 문장의 동사 시제를 확인하고 어법상 적절한 표현을 고르시오.

07   From various evidence found throughout Italy, the average height of the ancient Romans seems to be / have been very short.

08   She is ashamed of making / having made such a mistake last week.

to부정사·동명사의 의미상 주어 찾기

의미상 주어와 준동사는 주어-동사 관계이므로, 준동사의 태를 판단하려면 의미상 주어부터 정확히 찾아내야 한다. to부정사와 동명사의 의미상 주어는 대개 문장의 주어, 목적어 등 문장에 있는 어구와 일치하는데, 일반인(we, you 등)인 경우는 따로 표현하지 않는다.

의미상 주어가 문장에 없을 경우 따로 표기를 하므로 쉽게 알 수 있다.
It is rare **for sharks** **to attack** people. (상어가 사람을 공격하는 것은 드문 일이다.)
It is very cruel **of you** **to abuse** animals like that. (동물을 그렇게 학대하다니 너는 매우 잔인하다.)
I deeply appreciate **your** **doing** me a favor. (부탁을 들어주셔서 정말 감사합니다.)

다음 각 문장에서 굵게 표시된 준동사의 의미상 주어를 찾아 밑줄을 치시오. (의미상 주어가 일반인이어서 문장에 없는 것도 있음)

01 We expect **to hear** from Sally soon.

02 Music and lighting are used to encourage shoppers **to buy** more.

03 Fortunately, my dream **to direct** my own movie came true.

04 It's nice **to get up** in the morning, but it's nicer **to stay** in bed.

05 It wasn't easy for me **to travel** alone in India without spending much money.

06 I failed my driving test because I didn't practice **driving** in traffic enough.

07 Be sure to send letters thanking them for **dropping by**.

08 My favorite activity is **reading** detective stories.

09 **Learning** how to swim is a wonderful journey to enjoy.

10 I don't like his **borrowing** my things without asking.

11 I remember each one of them **saying** the same thing.

*동명사의 의미상 주어를 소유격으로 만들기 어려울 때는 목적격으로 나타낸다.

다음 중 어법상 적절한 표현을 고르시오.

01 In China it has never been rare for emperors to paint, but one king became so involved in painting that the entire Northern Song Dynasty is thought to fall / to have fallen because of it. [기출 응용]

02 도전 College life is busy. Too many demands on your schedule — such as clubs, friends, and parties — may cause some difficulties in your performance / performing compulsory tasks like homework. [기출 응용]

03 Ultrasound produces an image by bounce / bouncing sound waves off an object inside the body. A picture is then created using the reflected sound waves. [기출 응용]

04 Renaissance artists reformed painting. They wanted objects in paintings to represent / be represented with accuracy. [기출 응용]

05 Kept at room temperature, this red wine is best consumed within five days of the bottle opening / being opened .

다음 밑줄 친 부분이 어법상 올바르면 ○표, 틀리면 ✕표하고 바르게 고치시오.

06 One ancient Greek athlete is reported to <u>have eaten</u> dried figs to enhance training. There are also reports that marathon runners in the 1908 Olympics drank cognac to improve performance. [기출]

07 도전 In professional sports these days, players and coaches don't focus on the result itself. They talk about focusing on the process and following the process. They talk about the actions they need to <u>be taken</u> in order to achieve their desired result. [기출 응용]

우리말에 맞도록 괄호 안의 어구를 바르게 배열하시오. (어형 변화 가능, 한 단어 추가)

08 강하고 유연성 있는 종이로 만들어지기 위해, 식물 원료는 복잡한 과정을 거쳐야 한다.
(into, flexible, of paper, strong, sheets, make, and)

To _____ , the plant materials must undergo a complicated process.

to-v 자리인가, v-ing 자리인가

<예제> When she reached her car, it occurred to her that she might have forgotten ┃turning off / to turn off┃ the gas range. [기출 응용]

출제의도 to부정사와 동명사를 모두 목적어로 취하는 동사의 의미 구분하기

해결전략 목적어가 동사의 때보다 미래의 일을 뜻하면 to부정사, 현재나 과거의 일을 뜻하면 동명사를 쓴다.

to-v (v할 것을)	동사의 시점에서 아직 하지 않은 미래의 일
v-ing (v하는 것을, v한 것을)	동사의 시점과 동시의 일 또는 그보다 이전의 일

다음 괄호 안에 주어진 동사의 형태를 올바르게 변형해서 쓰시오.

01   Remember (brush) _____ your tongue when you brush your teeth. [기출 응용]

02   I remember (read) _____ the article in yesterday's newspaper.

03   Her high notes sounded like a gate which someone had forgotten (oil) _____ . [기출]

04   I will never forget (meet) _____ that legendary movie maker.

05   She's trying (learn) _____ more about the history of India.

06   He tried (send) _____ her flowers, but it didn't impress her much.

07   I regret (tell) _____ you that your team lost the match.

08   I don't regret (lend) _____ him money when he needed it.

09   He stopped (get) _____ a drink of water.

10   Suddenly the pianist stopped (play) _____ . No sound was heard.

• stop to-v의 to-v는 stop의 목적어가 아니라 'v하기 위해(목적)'를 나타내는 부사적 용법

Point Exercise

정답 및 해설 p. 13

다음 중 어법상 적절한 표현을 고르시오.

01 Remember to plug / plugging your cell phone into its charger when you go to bed, so you can use it all day tomorrow. [기출 응용]

02 The washing machine made a lot of noise, and later, it stopped to operate / operating entirely. [기출 응용]

03 I inadvertently passed what I thought was a rock in the road. When I stopped checking / to check it out, I discovered a little tortoise.

04 My grandma was a good singer when she was alive. I can't forget her to sing / singing gospel songs in her beautiful alto tone. [기출 응용]

05 I can remember (A) to feel / feeling very frustrated and confused sometimes in my teens. I can also remember my emotions (B) to swing / swinging from one extreme to another.

[기출 응용]

다음 밑줄 친 부분이 어법상 올바르면 ○표, 틀리면 ✕표하고 바르게 고치시오.

06 Since we know we can't completely eliminate our biases, we need to try to limit the harmful impacts they can have on the objectivity and rationality of our decisions and judgments.

[기출 응용]

우리말에 맞도록 괄호 안의 어구를 바르게 배열하시오. (어형 변화 가능, 주어진 어구로만 배열할 것)

07 4명 중 한 사람은 은퇴를 위해 생애에서 더 빨리 저축을 시작하지 않은 것을 후회한다.
(earlier in life, regret, not, for retirement, to, save, start)

One in four people _____.

to부정사를 목적어로 취하는 동사 vs. 동명사를 목적어로 취하는 동사

밑줄 어법 문제의 정답으로 빈출되는 것은 아니지만 오답 밑줄로 충분히 출제 가능성이 있고, 워낙 사용 빈도가 높아 어형 변화가 필요한 내신 영작 문제에도 감초처럼 등장하므로 확실히 정리하고 넘어가도록 하자.

1. 동사+to-v: v할 것을

to-v는 주로 미래, 즉 앞으로 하려고 하는 일, 아직 하지 못한 일을 뜻하는 경우가 많다.

can('t) afford *to-v*	expect *to-v*	offer *to-v*
agree *to-v*	fail *to-v* (v하지 못하다, v하지 않다)	plan *to-v*
arrange *to-v* (v하도록 마련하다, 처리하다)	hope *to-v*	pretend *to-v*
ask *to-v*	learn *to-v*	promise *to-v*
choose *to-v*	long *to-v*	refuse *to-v*
consent *to-v* (v하기로 동의하다)	manage *to-v* (간신히[용케] v해내다)	want *to-v*
decide *to-v*	mean *to-v* (v할 의도이다, v할 작정이다)	wish *to-v*
desire *to-v*	need *to-v*	would like *to-v*

2. 동사+v-ing: v하는 것을, v한 것을

v-ing는 주로 과거에 이미 해본 일, 현재 하는 일을 뜻하는 경우가 많다.

acknowledge *v-ing*	enjoy *v-ing*	postpone *v-ing*
admit *v-ing*	finish *v-ing*	practice *v-ing*
appreciate *v-ing* (v하는 것에 대해 감사하다)	forgive *v-ing*	put off *v-ing*
avoid *v-ing*	give up *v-ing*	quit *v-ing*
consider *v-ing*	imagine *v-ing*	recommend *v-ing*
delay *v-ing*	keep (on) *v-ing*	resist *v-ing*
deny *v-ing*	mention *v-ing*	risk *v-ing* (v하는 모험을 하다)
discuss *v-ing*	mean *v-ing* (v를 의미하다, v를 초래하다)	suggest *v-ing*
	mind *v-ing* (v하는 것을 꺼리다)	understand *v-ing*

다음 중 어법상 적절한 표현을 고르시오.

01   The revolution failed to turn / turning China into a truly independent and democratic country.

02   Julie and her husband are considering to adopt / adopting a second child.

03   The company has decided to remodel / remodeling the store very soon. [기출 응용]

04   The study revealed that more than 56% of gifted children managed to know / knowing the letters of the alphabet before they reached the age of 2 years.

05   The boy enjoyed wheeling / to wheel the grocery cart up and down the aisles of the supermarket as his mother collected the things for the shopping list. [기출 응용]

06   The spokesperson was unwilling to confirm or deny to have / having said such a thing.

07   Avoid to touch / touching a wounded wild animal even when you think it is safe to do so. The animal may attack you. [기출 응용]

08   A winning coach can't afford to let / letting little things go overlooked because that often means the difference between success and failure. [기출 응용]

09   David dreamed of being a football player, but his father refused to listen / listening to him, insisting that he go to medical school instead. [기출 응용]

10   Samuel suggested to call / calling the manufacturer to fix the broken printer.

감정 동사의 v-ing vs. p.p.

<예제> If you are constantly engaged in asking yourself questions about things you are hearing, you will find that even boring lecturers become a bit more interesting / interested , because much of the interest will be coming from what you are generating rather than what the lecturer is offering. [기출]

출제의도 감정 동사들의 능동, 수동 구분하기

해결전략 감정 동사의 의미상 주어가 누군가에게 감정을 유발하는 것이면 **v-ing**, 의미상 주어가 감정을 느끼는 것이면 **p.p.**를 쓴다.

v-ing	의미상 주어가 누군가에게 감정을 유발할 때
p.p.	의미상 주어가 감정을 느낄 때

[감정 동사] interest, surprise, excite, please, amaze, shock, depress, frustrate, embarrass, frighten, confuse, puzzle 등

다음 네모 안의 준동사의 의미상 주어에 밑줄을 긋고 어법상 적절한 표현을 고르시오.

01   The news was interesting / interested enough to draw my attention.

02   None of the players are interesting / interested in winning the championship.

03   I couldn't find anything that was pleasing / pleased to my eye.

04   Steven, pleasing / pleased by his own drawings, sent his best work to the contest.

05   Those in-depth analyses may turn out to be surprising / surprised .

06   People on vacation were surprising / surprised by the sudden cold weather.

Point Exercise

정답 및 해설 p. 14

다음 중 어법상 적절한 표현을 고르시오.

01   The results of the study conducted by health researchers were shocking / shocked . Doctors frequently failed to tell patients basic information about drugs and their potential side effects. [기출 응용]

02   Many of the art critics were surprising / surprised to see works tackling China's environmental problems and the economic difficulties experienced by many migrant workers.

03   The computer is amazing / amazed not because it can handle complex mathematical operations, but because it can perform them in one billionth of a second without error. [기출 응용]

04   Among twenty students, only three could read, and none could write. I felt quite depressing / depressed at the thought of the hard work ahead of me. [기출 응용]

05   Students interesting / interested in the position of president will talk to their classmates and make posters to let others know they are running for that office. [기출 응용]

다음 밑줄 친 부분이 어법상 올바르면 ○표, 틀리면 ✕표하고 바르게 고치시오.

06   We're heading toward a world where information fragments about us will be forever
도전   preserved on the Internet. This data can often be of dubious reliability; it can be false; or it can be true but deeply <u>humiliated</u>. [기출 응용]   *dubious: 의심스러운

우리말에 맞도록 괄호 안의 어구를 바르게 배열하시오. (어형 변화 가능, 주어진 어구로만 배열할 것)

07   내게, 개학 첫 주는 불확실성과 새로운 얼굴들로 인해 두려움을 주곤 했다.
    (of school, used to, the first week, be, frighten)

    To me, _____, with its uncertainties and new faces.

전치사 to + v-ing

<예제> A scientist left people in shock after telling them that an asteroid was likely to ｜hit / hitting｜ Earth.

출제의도 전치사 to의 목적어 자리와 to부정사 자리 구별하기

해결전략 네모나 밑줄 앞에 to가 있으면 전치사 to인지 부정사를 이끄는 to인지 확인한다.

to-v	• be likely to-v: v할 것 같다, v할 것으로 예상되다 • be sure[certain] to-v: 꼭[반드시] v하다 • be ready to-v: v할 준비가 되다 • be willing to-v: 기꺼이 v하다 • be reluctant to-v: v하기를 꺼리다 • be[feel] inclined to-v: v하고 싶다; v하는 경향이 있다 • be due to-v: v할 예정이다 　cf. due to+명사(구): ~ 덕분에, ~ 때문에 • be eager[anxious] to-v: v하고 싶어 하다
to v-ing / 명사(구)	• object to v-ing: v하는 것에 반대하다 • be opposed to v-ing: v하는 것에 반대하다 • look forward to v-ing: v하기를 고대하다 • be[get] used[accustomed] to v-ing: v하는 것에 익숙하다[익숙해지다] 　cf. be used to-v: v하는 데 사용되다 (☞ Testing Point 28 참조) • commit oneself to v-ing: v하는 데 헌신[전념]하다 (be committed to v-ing) • dedicate[devote] oneself to v-ing: v하는 데 헌신하다 　(be dedicated[devoted] to v-ing) • be addicted to v-ing: v하는 것에 중독되다 • adjust to v-ing: v하는 것에 적응하다 • when it comes to v-ing: v에 관한 한 • from A to B: A에서 B까지, A에서 B로 • close to: ~에 근접한

다음 중 어법상 적절한 표현을 고르시오.

01　Rose is due to ｜start / starting｜ school in January.

　　cf. The team's success was largely due to her efforts.

02　I'm not used to ｜use / using｜ chopsticks.

　　cf. Chopsticks are used to ｜grasp / grasping｜ food.

03　We have moved from going to a football game once a week to ｜have / having｜ sports on television 24 hours a day. [기출 응용]

Point Exercise

다음 밑줄 친 부분이 어법상 올바르면 ○표, 틀리면 ✕표하고 바르게 고치시오.

01   He had no problem enrolling boys but found that Indian mothers objected to <u>having</u> girls taken from home because they wanted to educate the girls themselves.

02   People look forward to <u>watch</u> women's gymnastics in particular. Girls and boys all around the world today look up to women athletes in the Olympics. [기출 응용]

03   When I returned to my hotel room after taking a lot of pictures, I was eager to <u>uploading</u> the photos to my blog. I plugged my digital camera into my computer, and when the process was complete, no photos were there! [기출 응용]

04   If farmers make a sudden change in what they feed their cows, the cows may lose a lot of weight. For this reason, a farmer should change a cow's diet slowly, so that it can get used to <u>eat</u> the new food. [기출 응용]

05   His book, *The Art of Travel*, covered every situation, from constructing boats, huts, and tents in a hurry to <u>catch</u> fish without a line. [기출 응용]

06   High-performing schools had faculty and staff who shared a vision of instructional purpose, who believed that all students could learn, and who committed themselves to <u>improve</u> students' academic performance.

07   Dog booties are a great idea, but many dogs take a while to adjust to <u>having</u> booties on, and it takes a lot of patience for the dogs to accept wearing them.

08   Fueled by a lifelong love of literature, Gonzales has devoted himself to <u>providing</u> people with more access to literature. [기출 응용]

to-v, v-ing를 포함하는 관용표현

CASE 1 to-v

01	make it a rule[point] to-v	v하기로 하고 있다, v하는 것을 원칙[규칙]으로 하다
	= make a rule[point] of v-ing	
02	have no choice but to-v	v하지 않을 수 없다
03	to begin with	우선, 첫째로
04	to say nothing of	~은 말할 것도 없이
	= not to speak of, not to mention	
05	needless to say	말할 나위도 없이, 물론
06	to tell the truth	사실은, 사실대로 말하자면
	= in fact, as a matter of fact	
07	to make matters worse	설상가상으로
08	so to speak	말하자면
09	to make[cut] a long story short	간단히 말하자면
	= to sum up, to put it briefly	
10	strange to say	이상하게 들리겠지만
11	not to say	~라고 말할 수는 없어도
12	to be sure	확실히

CASE 2 v-ing

01	There is no v-ing	v할 수 없다
02	It is no use v-ing	v해도 소용없다
	= It is of no use to-v	
03	feel like v-ing	v하고 싶은 생각이 들다
04	cannot help v-ing	v하는 것을 피할 수 없다, v하지 않을 수 없다
	= cannot help but v	
05	be worth v-ing	v할 가치가 있다
06	on v-ing	v하자마자
07	far from v-ing	전혀 v하는 것이 아닌, v하기는커녕
08	end up v-ing	결국 v하게 되다
09	spend ~ (in) v-ing	v하는 데 (시간, 비용 등을) 들이다, 쓰다
10	waste ~ (in) v-ing	v하는 데 (시간, 비용 등을) 낭비하다
11	have difficulty[trouble, a hard time] (in) v-ing	v하는 데 어려움을 겪다
12	keep[stop, prevent, prohibit] A from v-ing	A가 v하는 것을 막다

다음 밑줄 친 부분이 어법상 올바르면 ○표, 틀리면 ✕표하고 바르게 고치시오.

01 Meditation is based on the principle that if we try to ignore or repress unpleasant thoughts or sensations, then we only end up <u>to increase</u> their intensity. [기출 응용]

02 They had 57 young adults spend five minutes before bed <u>writing</u> either a to-do list for the days ahead or a list of tasks they'd finished over the past few days. [기출]

03 Today's laws prevent a U.S. president from <u>being</u> elected for more than two terms. [기출 응용]

04 Most graduates have difficulty <u>getting</u> a first job.

05 On his <u>opening</u> the front door, two dogs jumped down off the sofa and approached to greet him.

우리말에 맞도록 괄호 안의 어구를 바르게 배열하시오. (어형 변화 가능, 필요한 어구 추가 가능)

06 그것이 무엇인지를 이해하지 않고 무언가를 외우는 것은 소용이 없다.
(something, learn, use, by heart)

It _____ without understanding what it is.

07 나는 비가 많이 와서 내 여행을 취소할 수밖에 없었다.
(choice, cancel, my trip)

I _____ because of heavy rain.

08 전기가 우리 삶에서 많은 소중한 것들을 우리에게 제공해준다는 점은 부인할 수 없다.
(deny, many valuable things, with, that, supply, us, electricity, in our lives)

There _____ .

09 나는 네가 그것을 일부러 그랬다고밖에 생각할 수 없다.
(help, think, do, that, on purpose)

I _____ .

다음 밑줄 친 부분이 어법상 올바르면 ○표, 틀리면 ✕표하고 바르게 고치시오.

01
[도전]
As long as the machinery or employee training <u>needs</u> for productivity improvements costs less than the value of the productivity gains, it's an easy investment for any business to make.

[기출 응용]

02
When I was young, my parents worshipped medical doctors as if they were exceptional beings <u>possessing</u> godlike qualities. [기출]

03
Lions and tigers first eat the blood, hearts, livers, and brains of the animals they kill, often <u>leave</u> the muscle meat for eagles. These organs tend to be much higher in fat. [기출]

04
Around 3/4 of the energy is expended on neurons, the <u>specialized</u> brain cells that communicate in vast networks to generate our thoughts and behaviors. [기출]

05
<u>Facing</u> with a group of spear-wielding adversaries, we needed to know instantly whether there were more of them than us. [기출 응용]   *spear-wielding: 창을 휘두르는

06
Regardless of the type of information <u>disclosed</u>, clients must be certain that it will not be used against them in a court of law, by the authorities or by any other party. [기출]

07
Letters were normally carried overland in early modern Europe, but a system of transporting letters and newspapers, as well as people, by canal boat <u>to develop</u> in the Dutch Republic in the seventeenth century. [기출 응용]

08
An arctic explorer found that the Inuit were careful to save fatty meat and organs for human consumption while <u>giving</u> muscle meat to the dogs. In this way, humans ate as other large, meat-eating mammals eat. [기출 응용]

09
Though it is true that the overall use of energy is reduced during sleep, as <u>compared</u> with the active waking state, there is almost as much reduction in energy use from just resting quietly.

[기출]

10 The time doctors use to keep records is time they could have spent seeing patients. Because the time <u>spending</u> with their patients is worth a lot, the opportunity cost of record keeping for doctors will be high. [기출]

다음 문장에서 어법상 **틀린** 부분을 찾아 밑줄을 긋고 바르게 고치시오.

11 Koalas rest sixteen to eighteen hours a day and spend most of that unconscious. In fact, koalas spend little time thinking; their brains actually appear to shrink over the last few centuries. [기출]

12 The attraction the early humans had visually toward the nonhuman creatures inhabited their world becomes profoundly meaningful. Among hunter-gatherers, animals are not only good to eat, they are also good to think about. [기출 응용]

13 Aristotle explained that a stone falling through the air is due to the stone having the property of "gravity." But of course a piece of wood tossing into water floats instead of sinking. [기출]

14 About 250 years ago, fossil fuels began to be used on a large scale for powering machines of many different kinds, thereby created the virtually unlimited amounts of artificial complexity that we are familiar with today. [기출]

15
도전
The Internet and communication technologies play an ever-increasing role in the social lives of young people. Adolescents have been quick to immerse themselves in technology with most used the Internet to communicate. [기출]

다음 빈칸에 들어갈 말을 쓰시오.

❶ **문장구조** ▶ UNIT 01

- 한 문장에 접속사[관계사] 없이 두 개의 동사가 있으면 하나는 1 _____ 여야 한다.
  접속사[관계사]의 개수 + 1은 2 _____ 의 개수이다.
  동사는 주어의 동작이나 상태를 서술하며, 준동사는 문장에서 주어, 목적어, 보어, 수식어(구) 역할을 한다.
- 병렬구조를 이끄는 접속사와 구문을 알아두고, 정확한 문장 해석을 통해 문맥상 올바르게 연결되는 것을 찾아야 한다.

❷ **준동사** ▶ UNIT 02

- 3 _____ 와 분사를 주어, 동사의 관계로 놓고 능동, 수동을 판별한다.
- 준동사는 4 _____ 성질이 있으므로 목적어를 취할 수 있고 부사가 수식할 수 있다. 동사처럼 태와 시제를 나타낼 수도 있다. 의미상 주어와의 의미 관계를 살펴 태를 구분하고, 문장의 동사가 나타내는 때와의 전후 관계를 통해 알맞은 시제 형태를 판단한다.
- 준동사는 동사에서 나온 것이므로 5 _____ 로 수식한다.
- to부정사와 동명사를 모두 목적어로 취하는 동사인 경우, 목적어가 동사의 때보다 미래의 일을 뜻하면 6 _____, 현재나 과거의 일을 뜻하면 7 _____ 를 쓴다.
- 감정 동사의 의미상 주어가 누군가에게 감정을 유발하는 것이면 8 _____, 의미상 주어가 감정을 느끼는 것이면 9 _____ 를 쓴다.
  [감정 동사] interest, surprise, excite, please, amaze, shock, depress, frustrate, embarrass, frighten, confuse, puzzle 등
- 네모나 밑줄 앞에 to가 있으면 10 _____ to인지 부정사를 이끄는 to인지 확인한다.

다음 중 어법상 적절한 표현을 고르시오.

01 Although the exact function of the ancient maps is unknown, the discovery makes one thing certain: humans have long desired to represent / be represented their physical surroundings. [기출 응용]

02 Birth order may define your role within a family, but as you mature into adulthood, accepted / accepting other social roles, birth order becomes insignificant. [기출]

03 Some of the obvious signs that a person is depressing / depressed are persistent feelings in that person of sadness, guilt, fear, and pain.

04 Consider what happens in public schools in December just before the winter break. Kids get sick. Teachers get sick. Parents get sick. We tend to think there are just a lot of viruses go / going around. [기출]

05 [도전] The costs of providing first-rate education just keep going up. We've done everything we can contain / to contain costs without compromising quality. One of those things is to set up a scholarship fund for students with special financial needs. [기출]

06 Taking early action to fix a problem is better than ignoring it and hoping / to hope it will go away and get better on its own. [기출 응용]

07 Researchers asked 32 people to watch a brief computer animation of white bars drifting over a grey and black background and say / said which way they were moving. [기출]

08 Hairdressers are constantly servicing clients who come in with a picture clipped from a beauty magazine and tell / telling the stylist, "This is the look I want — cut my hair like this." [기출 응용]

다음 밑줄 친 부분이 어법상 올바르면 ○표, 틀리면 ✕표하고 바르게 고치시오.

09 A short move may seem easy, but it will still take several trips. There is also the possibility of <u>damage</u> your stuff, some of it valuable. [기출 응용]

10 "Working memory," or "short-term memory," is a term <u>using</u> to describe the fact that one can hold only a limited amount of material in one's mind at one time. [기출 응용]

11 Breathing has a price. The combustion of oxygen that keeps us alive and active <u>sending</u> out by-products called oxygen free radicals. [기출]

*oxygen free radical: 활성 산소

12 Many small mammals living in cold climates, who lose heat easily by having an unfavorable surface area to body weight ratio, <u>tending</u> to sleep a lot, often in insulating burrows. [기출]

13 Pets are important in the treatment of <u>depressed</u> or chronically ill patients. [기출]

14 At first, it was really hard and <u>frustrated</u> to be thousands of miles away from home, studying alone abroad.

15 The system of transporting letters and newspapers in the Dutch Republic allowed communication not only between Amsterdam and smaller towns, but also between one small town and another, thus <u>equalized</u> accessibility to information. [기출 응용]

16 The general was determined not to allow the enemy's forces a return voyage, but to send them to the bottom of the sea. <u>Stood high</u> on his warship, he led his entire fleet into a battle with several hundred enemy ships. [기출 응용]

17 Three hours later we saw a small boy, dressed in rags and with long hair <u>fallen</u> down his back, herding camels. He led us to the Bait Imani camp.

18 도전 Some heroes shine in the face of great adversity, performing amazing deeds in difficult situations; other heroes, unnoticed by most of us, do their work quietly, <u>made</u> a difference in the lives of other people. [기출 응용]

19 Some bees take advantage of the hard work of others. They sneak into the nest of an <u>unsuspected</u> "normal" bee (known as the host), lay an egg near the pollen mass being gathered by the host bee for her own offspring, and then sneak back out. [기출 응용]

20   The lack of real, direct experience in and with nature has caused many children to regard the natural world as mere abstraction, that fantastic, beautifully filmed place <u>filled</u> with endangered rainforests and polar bears in peril. [기출 응용]

*peril: 위험

21   Metacognition simply means "thinking about thinking," and it is one of the main distinctions between the human brain and that of other species. Our ability to stand high on a ladder above our normal thinking processes and <u>evaluate</u> why we are thinking as we are thinking is an evolutionary marvel. [기출]

다음 밑줄 친 부분 중에서 어법상 **틀린** 부분을 찾아 기호를 쓰고 바르게 고치시오.

22   People from more individualistic cultural contexts tend (A) <u>to be motivated</u> to maintain self-focused agency or control as this serves as the basis of one's self-worth. With this form of agency comes the belief that individual successes (B) <u>depending</u> primarily on one's own abilities and actions, and thus, whether by influencing the environment or trying to accept one's circumstances, the use of control ultimately centers on the individual. [기출 응용]

23   During the early stages when the aquaculture industry was rapidly expanding, mistakes were made. High-density rearing led to outbreaks of infectious diseases that in some cases (A) <u>devastated</u> not just the caged fish, but local wild fish populations too. The negative impact on local wildlife inhabiting areas close to the fish farms (B) <u>continues</u> to be an ongoing public relations problem for the industry. Furthermore, a general lack of knowledge and insufficient care being taken when fish pens were initially constructed (C) <u>meaning</u> that pollution from excess feed and fish waste created huge barren underwater deserts. [기출 응용]

PART

II

Relatives, Conjunctions & Prepositions

Testing Point 08   관계사의 기본 역할

전체 기출 빈도   ♦♦♦♦♦
최근 기출 빈도   ♦♦♦♦♦

<예제> The island was taken by the English, | who / whom | restored it the following year to the French by the Peace of Paris. [기출 응용]

출제의도 관계사의 역할과 쓰임 구분하기

해결전략 관계사는 절과 절을 연결하는 접속사 역할을 하면서 관계사절 내에서 대명사/부사의 역할을 한다.

관계대명사 who, which, whose, whom, that	관계대명사의 격은 관계대명사가 관계대명사절에서 대신하는 문장 요소와 일치한다. • 주어를 대신하면 주격(who, which, that) • 목적어를 대신하면 목적격(who(m), which, that) • 소유를 나타내는 his, her 등을 대신하면 소유격(whose 또는 of which)

• 기본적인 사항으로서, 사람이 선행사이면 who[that], whom, whose를 쓰고 사람 이외의 선행사는 which[that], whose를 써야 한다.

다음 밑줄 친 부분에서 빠져 있는 문장 요소를 확인하고 그 요소와 일치하는 관계대명사의 격을 고르시오.

01   Visitors | who / whom | came all the way from Canada will gather here.

02   James married a Japanese girl | whose / whom | he met on the Internet.

03   People | who / whose | families came from China account for half of the population.

• 콤마와 관계사

제한적 용법: 앞에 콤마가 없으며 선행사를 수식, 제한하는 형용사절을 이끈다.

Green onion is *a plant* **that** you can regrow easily. (파는 쉽게 다시 키울 수 있는 식물이다.)

계속적 용법: 앞에 콤마가 있으며 선행사에 대한 부가 정보를 나타내는 절을 이끈다. that은 계속적 용법으로 쓰지 않는다. which는 단어뿐 아니라 어구, 절도 선행사로 할 수 있다.

The groom wears *a tuxedo*, **which** is commonly rented just for his wedding day. [기출 응용]
(신랑은 턱시도를 입는데, 그것은 보통 자신의 결혼식날만을 위해서 빌리는 것이다.)

He tried to persuade his mom, **which** made him more ill at ease than ever.
(그는 엄마를 설득하려고 애썼는데, 그것이 그를 그 어느 때보다도 더 불편하게 했다.)

관계부사 when, where, why, how	관계부사절 내에서 관계부사는 '때, 장소, 이유, 방법'을 선행사로 하여 부사로 쓰인다. • how는 선행사 the way나 how 중 하나를 반드시 생략한다.

다음 문장에서 선행사를 찾아 밑줄을 긋고 어법상 적절한 표현을 고르시오.

04   There was a time | when / where | prices were almost constant.

05   The city | when / where | he lives is by the sea.

06   There is no reason | where / why | they should be here.

07   This is how[the way] you do it.

• 관계대명사의 선행사는 현대 영어에서 생략이 거의 일어나지 않으나, 관계부사 when, where, why의 선행사가 매우 일반적인 것(the time, the day, the place, the reason 등)일 때는 생략되기도 한다.
  She didn't tell me (the time) **when** she was arriving. (그녀는 나에게 도착할 시간을 말해 주지 않았다.)
  He lives about five blocks away from (the place) **where** I live. (그는 내가 사는 곳에서 다섯 블록 떨어진 곳에 산다.)
• 계속적 용법으로 쓰일 수 있는 것은 when, where이고 나머지는 쓰지 않는다.

대명사 vs. 관계대명사	관계대명사 = 접속사+대명사 • 대명사는 절과 절을 연결할 수 없고 관계대명사와 중복해서 쓸 수도 없다.
부사 vs. 관계부사	관계부사 = 접속사+부사(구) • 부사(구)는 절과 절을 연결할 수 없고 관계부사와 중복해서 쓸 수도 없다.

다음 중 어법상 적절한 표현을 고르시오.

08   She showed me around her house, | it / which | was so cozy.

09   Europe has 250 minority languages, many of | them / which | are unofficial.

10   We left at five, | then / when | the gate was closed.

11   When Einstein was ten, his family enrolled him in the Luitpold Gymnasium, | there / where | he came
     to possess a suspicion of authority. [기출 응용]

• **many of + 관계대명사**
  many of, all of, both of, some of, one of, none of, most of, half of 등의 어구는 관계대명사 앞에 자주 놓인다.
  I don't like *the food* at the restaurant, **most of *which*** was not very good.
  → I don't like *the food* at the restaurant. + **Most of *the food*** was not very good.
     (나는 그 식당의 음식을 좋아하지 않는데, 대부분의 음식은 별로 맛있지 않았다.)

다음 중 어법상 적절한 표현을 고르시오.

❶ In law, an alien is a person in a country who / which is not a national of that country.

❷ He quit his teaching job and moved to Hempstead, an epicenter for young writers at the time, when / where he worked in a used book store.

❸ Businesses perceive as competitors a narrow range of the business world; there are many cases how / where they don't understand their real rivals.

❹ When she was twenty, she married a man who / whom she believed was her knight in shining armor. He was a dream come true.

❺ I discovered that it was still possible to observe and live with people who utilized a stone tool and who / which relied on traditional products for their daily lives.

Guides

① ② 선행사의 위치

선행사는 대부분 관계사 바로 앞에 위치하지만 선행사를 뒤에서 수식하는 어구나 삽입어구가 있을 수 있기 때문에 주의해야 한다. 선행사는 관계사절이 수식 또는 보충 설명하는 것으로 문맥이 자연스러운 것을 선택해야 한다.

③ 관계부사 where

'a city, a building' 등의 '장소'뿐 아니라, point(점), case(경우), circumstance(상황, 사정), situation(상황), stage(단계) 등과 같이 넓은 의미의 '장소'로 생각될 수 있는 단어를 선행사로 할 때도 쓰인다.

④ 주격 관계대명사 뒤의 I think류 (☞ p. 15 Guides 참조)

주격 관계대명사 뒤에 I think[believe, suppose] 등이 삽입되는 경우, 주격이 아닌 목적격 관계대명사가 되어야 하는 것으로 혼동할 수 있으므로 주의해야 한다.

아래 두 문장은 의미는 같으나 관계대명사의 격이 다르다.

These guys **who** (I thought) were my friends / are just like my parents.
      S′   V′   C′

These guys **who(m)** I thought ● (to be) my friends / are just like my parents.
        O′   S′ V′   C′

(내가 친구라고 생각했던 이 사람들은 내 부모님과 꼭 같다.)

⑤ 여러 개의 관계대명사절이 나오는 경우

관계대명사절이 여러 개가 겹쳐 나오는 경우 선행사를 제대로 파악해야 한다. 문맥상 관계대명사절이 수식하는 것으로 자연스러운 것을 찾으면 된다.

There's *a place* **that** I know **that** has the same name.

(내가 아는, 이름이 똑같은 장소가 하나 있다.)

Tea contains *chemicals* **which** shut down *a molecule* **that** can trigger the development of cancer.

(차에는 암 진행을 촉진시키는 어떤 분자를 차단하는 화학 물질들이 함유되어 있다.)

Tea contains *chemicals* **which** are antioxidants and **whose** biological activities may be relevant to

cancer prevention.

(차에는 산화 방지제이면서 그 자체의 생물학적 활동이 암 예방과 관련이 있을 수 있는 화학 물질들이 함유되어 있다.)

Point Exercise

정답 및 해설 p. 21

다음 중 어법상 적절한 표현을 고르시오.

01 Most professors see themselves in a position of professional authority over their students
[함정] | who / which | they earned by many years of study. [기출 응용]

02 It is outrageous to spend that huge amount of money on a golf facility | which / whom | only a few will have access to. [기출 응용]

03 My son, | who / whose | dream is to be a *National Geographic* photographer, often takes me to the most photogenic places. [기출 응용]

04 I recently watched a news interview with an acquaintance | who / whom | I was certain was
[함정] going to lie about a few particularly sensitive issues. [기출 응용]

05 Many countries have laws | that / whose | limit fishing in certain areas and forbid the catching of endangered species. [기출 응용]

06 The skillful mechanic of the gas station has been replaced by a teenager in a uniform
| who / which | doesn't know anything about cars. [기출 응용]

07 In 1952, Ralph Ellison published the novel *Invisible Man*, | which / who | immediately
[함정] received praise from critics when published and won the National Book Award in 1953.

[기출 응용]

08 The animals (A) | whose / which | prey on zebras are busiest during the cool hours of sunrise and sunset. It turns out that the black and white stripes show up as grey from a distance,
(B) | which / that | helps the zebras blend with the low light. [기출]

다음 밑줄 친 부분이 어법상 올바르면 ○표, 어색하면 ✕표하고 바르게 고치시오.

09   Farms are a major source of a powerful greenhouse gas called methane, <u>it</u> is produced during the digestion of plants by animals, such as cattle and sheep.

10   An American geochemist, Clair Patterson, announced in 1965 that highly toxic lead could be found essentially everywhere on Earth, including in our own bodies, <u>who</u> helped launch the environmental movement to get rid of dangers such as lead paint.

11   It's a good thing, not a selfish thing, to choose people who are good for you. It's appropriate and praiseworthy to associate with people <u>whose</u> lives would be improved if they saw your life improve. [기출 응용]

12   This full-time intern position is designed for current law students who share a passion for justice and a healthy environment and <u>which</u> are seeking academic credit for the winter/ spring academic term.

우리말에 맞도록 괄호 안의 어구를 바르게 배열하시오. (어형 변화 가능, 필요한 어구 추가 가능)

13   한 빈민가에서, 어떤 문화 센터가 지역 아동들에게 음악 행사들을 무대에 올리도록 했는데, 그중 어떤 것들은 그 아동들이 아직 회복 중에 있었던 비극을 극화했다. [기출 응용]

(still, the tragedy, recover, the kids, dramatize, some of, from)

In one slum area, a culture center encouraged the local kids to stage musical events,

_____.

<예제> It is no coincidence that countries where / which sleep time has declined most dramatically over the past century are also those suffering the greatest increase in rates of physical diseases and mental disorders. [기출 응용]

출제의도 관계대명사와 관계부사의 쓰임 구분하기

해결전략 관계대명사 뒤에는 불완전한 절, 관계부사 뒤에는 완전한 절이 온다.

완전한 절	주어와 동사 외에도 동사가 필요로 하는 필수 요소인 목적어, 보어가 빠짐없이 갖춰진 절을 뜻한다. 물론 1문형은 주어, 동사만으로도 완전한 절을 이루고 2문형은 목적어 없이 보어만으로 완전한 절을 이룬다.

다음 문장이 완전한 절이면 ○표, 불완전한 절이면 주어, 동사, 목적어, 보어 중 무엇이 빠져 있는지를 빈칸에 쓰시오.

01   Works well with her colleagues. _____

02   A good leader is a good listener. _____

03   I need someone to help me out. _____

04   The doctor me some medicine. _____

05   I thought him. _____

관계대명사 vs. 관계부사[전치사+관계대명사]	<관계대명사+불완전한 절> <관계부사[전치사+관계대명사]+완전한 절>

다음 밑줄 친 부분이 완전한 절이면 ○표, 불완전한 절이면 주어와 목적어 중 무엇이 빠져 있는지를 빈칸에 쓰고 어법상 적절한 표현을 고르시오.

06   This is the photo which / where shows my family. _____

07   Tell me about the person when / who you respect most. _____

08   The yellow police tape marked the spot which / where a gun was found. _____

09   Remember the days which / when we feared nothing. _____

10   I cannot remember the reason who / why I lost my temper. _____

11   This book tells you whom / how our nervous system works. _____

• **소유격 관계대명사:** <소유격 관계대명사+명사>를 제외한 구조가 불완전하다.
  Firefighters are people **whose job** is to put out fires. (소방관은 불을 끄는 일을 하는 사람들이다.)

• **전치사+관계대명사:** 수식어구인 <전치사+명사>를 대신하므로, 관계부사와 같이 뒤에 완전한 절이 온다.
  Sawyer is the man **with whom** I play badminton every Saturday. (Sawyer는 내가 토요일마다 함께 배드민턴을 치는 그 남자이다.)
  (← Sawyer is the man. + I play badminton **with him** every Saturday.)
                         완전한 절

복합관계대명사	who(m)ever, whosever, whichever, whatever	<복합관계대명사+불완전한 절> 문장에서 명사절이나 부사절을 이끈다.		

주격	소유격	목적격	명사절	부사절
whoever	whosever	whomever	anyone who ~ (~하는 누구든지)	no matter who ~ (누가 ~하더라도)
whichever	—	whichever	any (one) that ~ (~하는 어느 쪽이든지)	no matter which ~ (어느 쪽을 ~하더라도)
whatever	—	whatever	any(thing) that ~ (~하는 것은 무엇이든지)	no matter what ~ (무엇을 ~하더라도)

복합관계부사	whenever, wherever, however	<복합관계부사+완전한 절> 문장에서 부사절을 이끈다.

	부사절	
whenever	at any time when ~ (~하는 언제든지)	no matter when ~ (언제 ~하더라도)
wherever	in any place where ~ (~하는 어디든지)	no matter where ~ (어디에 ~하더라도)
however	—	no matter how ~ (아무리 ~하더라도)

다음 밑줄 친 부분이 완전한 절이면 ○표, 불완전한 절이면 주어와 목적어 중 무엇이 빠져 있는지를 빈칸에 쓰고 어법상 적절한 표현을 고르시오.

12 Whoever / Whenever comes is welcome. _____

13 Whoever / Whenever I come to this restaurant, I order spaghetti. _____

14 You may change your name to wherever / whatever you like. _____

15 This phone will keep you connected wherever / whichever life takes you. _____

16 Whatever / However happens, always remain calm and centered. _____

17 Whatever / However great the photos are, they still need some editing here and there.

_____

- <whichever/whatever+명사>의 구조로, 형용사적으로도 쓰일 수 있다.
  You may take **whichever** *course* you like. (명사절: any course that)
  (좋아하는 어떤 과정이든 택해도 된다.)
  He offered **whatever** *help* he could give. (명사절: any help that)
  (그는 자신이 줄 수 있는 어떤 도움이든 제공했다.)
  We'll get there by five **whichever** *train* we take. (부사절: no matter which)
  (우리가 어떤 기차를 타더라도 그곳에 5시까지 도착할 것이다.)
  Whatever *results* follow, I will do my best. (부사절: no matter what)
  (어떤 결과가 따르더라도 나는 최선을 다할 것이다.)

- however 뒤의 문장 구조
  However **you do it**, the result will be the same. (네가 아무리 해도 결과는 같을 것이다.)
  However **nice he is**, he wouldn't do that. (그가 아무리 착해도 그것을 하려고 하지 않을 것이다.)
  However **carefully I explained**, she didn't understand. (내가 아무리 잘 설명해도 그녀는 이해하지 못했다.)

다음 중 어법상 적절한 표현을 고르시오.

❶ The Castle Inn, where / which I ran for ten years, was located in a quiet village with a loving community.

❷ As she lived in a small house, where / which she could not practice without disturbing the rest of the family, she usually practiced her high notes outside. [기출 응용]

Guides

❶ 다양한 문형에 쓰이는 동사

일부 동사들은 여러 문형으로 쓰일 수 있으므로 문맥과 구조를 고려하여 완전한 절인지 불완전한 절인지를 판단해야 한다.

Her mother **ran** a convenience store for 3 years. (~을 운영하다)

(그녀의 어머니는 편의점을 3년간 운영했다.)

He **ran** to the station to catch the last train. (달리다)

(그는 막차를 잡기 위해 역으로 달렸다.)

❷ 자동사와 타동사가 다 되는 동사

관계사절이 어떤 선행사를 수식하는 것이 자연스러운지를 따져서 완전한 절인지 불완전한 절인지를 판단하여야 한다.

The team is **practicing** for their big game on Friday.

(그 팀은 금요일에 있을 큰 시합을 위해 연습 중이다.)

They **practiced** *the dance* until it was perfect.

(그들은 완벽해질 때까지 그 춤을 연습했다.)

Point Exercise

정답 및 해설 p. 23

다음 중 어법상 적절한 표현을 고르시오.

01 In most cases [where / which] a problem arises in achieving our goals, I believe that communications either are part of the problem or are the source of the problem.

02 The most common reason to give flowers is to express romantic love. Nervous first dates, weddings, anniversaries, and Valentine's Day are occasions [when / which] cry out for beautiful, carefully selected flowers. [기출 응용]

03 According to the study, violence and property crimes occurred twice as often in apartment blocks [where / which] trees were few. [기출 응용]

04 The number of children suffering from allergies is increasing, and high standards of hygiene may be to blame. Dr. Levy longs for the old days [when / which] a child built a strong immune system by getting dirty. [기출 응용]

05 도전 Baseball has no set length of time within which the game must be completed. The game belongs to the kind of world [which / in which] people did not say, "I haven't got all day."

[기출 응용]

06 Some programs require students to follow clinical guidelines [whichever / whenever] they work in the lab.

07 도전 Women in that class did not usually dress themselves, but were dressed by maids. Since a maid would be facing a woman she was dressing, dress makers put the buttons on the maid's right, and this, of course, put them on the woman's left, [which / where] they have remained.

다음 중 어법상 적절한 표현을 고르시오.

01 The number one characteristic of successful entrepreneurs who / which will be a challenge for us to acquire is that they are risk-takers.

02 How is it possible to make sense of a situation which / in which the single word "uncle" applies to the brother of one's father and to the brother of one's mother? [기출]

다음 밑줄 친 부분이 어법상 올바르면 ○표, 틀리면 ×표하고 바르게 고치시오.

03 Hypnosis can put the brain into a special state <u>which</u> the powers of memory are dramatically greater than normal. [기출 응용]

04 The speed <u>at which</u> sound travels depends on the density of the medium which it is traveling through. [기출]

05 Humans are the only species on this planet that has constructed forms of complexity that use external energy sources. This was a fundamental new development, <u>for which</u> there were no precedents in history. [기출 응용]

06 Before the washing machine was invented, people used washboards to scrub, or they carried their laundry to riverbanks and streams <u>which</u> they beat and rubbed it against rocks. [기출 응용]

07 Confirmation bias is not the same as being stubborn, and is not constrained to issues <u>about which</u> people have strong opinions. [기출 응용]

08 Beginning in the 2nd Century A.D., Taoist and Confucian scholars engaged in a practice known as 'pure talk,' <u>which</u> they debated spiritual and philosophical issues before audiences in contests that might last for a day and a night. [기출]

09 Why do we often feel that others are paying more attention to us than they really are? The spotlight effect means seeing ourselves at center stage, thus intuitively overestimating the extent which others' attention is aimed at us. [기출]

10 The present moment feels special. It is real. However much you may remember the past or anticipate the future, you live in the present. Of course, the moment during which you read a sentence is no longer happening. [기출]

11 도전
Individuals with cruel or overly-competitive personalities may be successful to a certain extent, but they can eventually destroy an organization by driving away its most capable members. That is how a good-natured personality is worth far more than impressive academic training or technical ability.

12 Modern dentistry began in the 1700s in France. That was which Pierre Fauchard published his book called *The Surgeon Dentist*. It was the first book about dental science. [기출 응용]

13 도전
After six months, the toys made landfall on beaches near Inuvik, Canada, 3,000 kilometers from which they were lost. [기출 응용]   *landfall: (오랜 항해·비행 후) 처음 도착하는 육지; 상륙, 착륙

14 Not all organisms are able to find sufficient food to survive, so starvation is a kind of disvalue often found in nature. It also is part of the process of selection by which biological evolution functions. [기출]

관계사, 접속사와 전치사
RELATIVES, CONJUNCTIONS & PREPOSITIONS

Testing Point 10 　헷갈리는 what, that, which 완벽 정리

전체 기출 빈도 　◆◆◆◆◆
최근 기출 빈도 　◆◆◆◆◆

<예제> Many people do not understand (A) │ that / what │ hypnosis is a natural phenomenon. It is an altered state (B) │ that / what │ we frequently go into and out of. [기출 응용]

출제의도 접속사와 관계대명사의 쓰임 구분과 관계대명사끼리의 쓰임 구분하기

해결전략 what과 that[which]은 뒤에 절이 완전한지 불완전한지와 앞에 선행사나 콤마 유무에 따라 판단한다.

what	<관계대명사 what+불완전한 절> = 문장에서 주어, 목적어, 보어가 되는 명사절 (선행사를 포함하므로 앞에 선행사가 없다.) • 관계대명사 what은 콤마 뒤에 계속적 용법으로 쓸 수 없다.
that [which]	<접속사 that+완전한 절> = 명사절/동격절/부사절
	<관계대명사 that[which]+불완전한 절> (앞에 선행사가 있다.) • 관계대명사 that은 콤마 뒤에 계속적 용법으로 쓸 수 없고 which는 쓸 수 있다.

01 　　　┌── 주어가 없어 불완전 ──┐
　　What *makes leaders different* is that they act. [선행사 없음]
　　　　└ 주어 ┘

02 　You must not forget **what** ┌─목적어가 없어 불완전─┐
　　I'm going to tell you. [선행사 없음]
　　　　　　　　└ 동사 forget의 목적어 ┘

03 　The result was **what** ┌목적어가 없어 불완전┐
　　I had expected. [선행사 없음]
　　　　　　└ 보어 ┘

04 　I'm satisfied with **what** ┌목적어가 없어 불완전┐
　　he has done. [선행사 없음]
　　　　└ 전치사 with의 목적어 ┘

05 　We believe **that** ┌── SVO 구조로서 완전 ──┐
　　our taste in music expresses our individuality.
　　　　　└ 동사 believe의 목적어인 명사절 ┘

06 　There's a rumor **that** ┌SV 구조로서 완전┐
　　they broke up.
　　　└ = (동격절) ┘

07 　They spoke with **such** a strong country accent **that** ┌── SV 구조로서 완전 ──┐
　　I could hardly communicate with them.
　　　　　　　　　　　　└ 부사절 ┘

08 　What are *scientific principles* **that[which]** ┌─ 주어가 없어 불완전 ─┐
　　appear in everyday life? [선행사 있음/콤마 없음]

다음 밑줄 친 부분이 완전한 절이면 ○표, 불완전한 절이면 주어와 목적어 중 무엇이 빠져 있는지를 빈칸에 쓰고 어법상 적절한 표현을 고르시오.

09 He thought receiving praise for doing what / that obviously was the right thing would be totally inappropriate. [기출 응용] _____

10 Following your instincts could lead you to make impulsive decisions what / that you may regret later. [기출 응용] _____

- **it ~ that 강조구문**: 부사(구[절])를 강조하는 경우를 제외하고 that절은 불완전하다.

I met Hayden at the park. → It was / that **met Hayden at the park.** [주어가 없어 불완전]
  S V   O   부사구
                   It was *Hayden* that **I met at the park.** [목적어가 없어 불완전]
                   It was *at the park* that **I met Hayden.** [SVO 구조로서 완전]

어법 적용하기

다음 중 어법상 적절한 표현을 고르시오.

❶ Jackson Pollock developed that / what he called a "direct method," applying the paint directly onto an empty canvas.

❷ If nobody is waiting, you know that / what the bus just left — and you might have to wait 20 more minutes.

❸ This semester will be a lot different in that / which you will spend the whole time working on a research project.

Guides

❶❷ **완전한 절 vs. 불완전한 절**
UNIT 03에서 살펴보았듯이 동사마다 취할 수 있는 문형이 있으므로 문맥과 구조를 잘 판단해야 한다.
특히 SVOO와 SVOC(명사 보어) 문형에서 목적어가 없는데 완전한 절로 오판하기 쉽고, 목적어가 보이지 않는 SV, SVC 문형을 불완전한 절로 오판하기 쉬우므로 주의해야 한다.

❸ **that절은 전치사의 목적어가 될 수 없다.**
같은 명사절을 이끌지만 관계대명사 what절과 다르게 that절은 전치사의 목적어가 될 수 없다.
단, 아래의 경우는 예외이다.
This document is important **in that** it proves your innocence.
                    = ~이라는 점에서, ~이므로
(이 서류는 너의 결백을 증명한다는 점에서 중요하다.)
This house is perfect **except that** it costs too much money.
              = ~이라는 것 이외는
(이 집은 너무 비싸다는 것만 제외하면 완벽하다.)

Point Exercise

정답 및 해설 p. 25

다음 중 어법상 적절한 표현을 고르시오.

01 The earliest map is considered to have been made in 7000 B.C. in an ancient city that was in what / which is now present-day Turkey. [기출 응용]

02 Most customers have responded positively to the new cellphone models that / what allow you to see the person you are talking to. [기출 응용]

03 One way to learn about maps is to choose an area which / what you want to map out and make your own by yourself. [기출 응용]

04 You may have seen an entire school of fish suddenly change direction as one unit. That / What appears to us as simultaneous is actually a kind of "follow your neighbor" behavior moving faster than the eye can see. [기출 응용]

05 Many social scientists have believed for some time that / what birth order directly influences both personality and achievement in adult life. [기출 응용]

06 Old windows are often thicker at the bottom than at the top. The reason for this is that / what in the past, making uniformly flat glass was almost impossible. [기출 응용]

07 도전 Sociologists at Columbia University claim that we only like the music we listen to because we know others enjoy it. Using a specially developed website, they discovered that people were more likely to select that / what the website claimed were favorite choices. [기출 응용]

08 Vicky is on stage practicing for tomorrow night's performance of a play. The play is part of her high school's annual concert (A) that / what celebrates the end of the school year and shows (B) that / what the students have learned. [기출 응용]

다음 밑줄 친 부분이 어법상 올바르면 ○표, 틀리면 ×표하고 바르게 고치시오.

09 We might hear a song on the radio for the first time that catches our interest. Then the next time we hear it, we hear a lyric we didn't catch the first time, or we might notice <u>what</u> the piano or drums are doing in the background. [기출]

10 [도전] People seeking legal advice should be assured, when discussing their rights or obligations with a lawyer, <u>which</u> the latter will not disclose to third parties the information provided. [기출]

11 One wonders whether our children's inherent capacity to recognize, classify, and order information about their environment — abilities once essential to our very survival — is slowly devolving to facilitate life in their increasingly virtualized world. It's all part of <u>what</u> Robert Pyle first called "the extinction of experience." [기출]

*devolve: 퇴화하다

다음 밑줄 친 부분 중 어법상 **틀린** 것을 찾아 기호를 쓰고 바르게 고치시오.

12 The body has many different parts (A) <u>that</u> work together to allow us to breathe, move, see, and digest food all at the same time. Most of the time we are unaware of (B) <u>that</u> is happening in our bodies. It is only when we get sick or feel pain that we notice it. [기출 응용]

13 There are two kinds of culture. One is material culture, (A) <u>which</u> is made up of physical objects (B) <u>that</u> people make and give meaning to, such as books and clothing. The other is non-material culture, consisting of human creations (C) <u>what</u> are abstract, like values and customs. [기출 응용]

우리말에 맞도록 괄호 안의 어구를 바르게 배열하시오. (어형 변화 가능, 필요한 어구 추가 가능, 중복 사용 가능)

14 레오나르도 다빈치는 비범한 머리와 남들이 보지 못하는 것을 보는 묘한 능력을 가지고 있었다.
(see, others)

Leonardo da Vinci had an unusual mind and an uncanny ability _____

_____ .

*uncanny: 묘한, 이상한

명사절과 부사절을 이끄는 기타 접속사

1. 명사절 접속사: whether[if], 의문사

(1) 접속사 that과 관계대명사 what 외에, 접속사 whether[if](~인지 (아닌지))나 의문사도 명사절을 이끌 수 있다.
명사절은 문장에서 주어, 목적어, 보어가 되거나 동격절에 해당한다.

> 관계대명사 what/의문대명사+불완전한 절
> 접속사/의문부사   +완전한 절

Every day people judge all other people. The question is **whether** they judge wisely. [보어절]
(날마다 사람들은 다른 모든 사람들을 판단한다. 문제는 그들이 현명하게 판단하는지 아닌지이다.)

cf. School uniforms make all the students look the same **whether** they are rich or not.
(학교 교복은 학생들이 부자든 아니든 간에 그들을 똑같아 보이게 한다.) (whether 부사절: ~이든 아니든)
The disease is curable **if** it is treated early.
(그 질병은 조기에 치료하면 완치될 수 있다.) (if 부사절: ~하면)

(2) 의문사가 접속사로서 명사절을 이끌기도 한다. 이 경우 어순(의문사+(S)+V)에 주의한다.
I can't tell *how many visitors* **I've had**. (얼마나 많은 방문객들이 왔는지 알 수 없다.)
I wonder *why* she's so mean to me. (왜 그녀가 나한테 그렇게 심술궂게 대하는지 궁금하다.)
Nobody knows *who* will win! (누가 이길지는 아무도 모른다!)

2. 부사절 접속사: 시간, 조건, 이유, 양보 (when/while, as, if/unless, because, since, (al)though 등)

(1) 완전한 구조의 절을 이끈다. 문장에서 주어, 목적어, 보어가 되는 명사절은 문장의 주요 요소에 해당하므로 생략하면 문장이
성립하지 않지만, 부사절은 생략해도 나머지 절만으로 문장이 성립한다는 차이점이 있다.

(2) 부사절의 주어가 주절의 주어와 일치하는 경우 부사절의 <주어+be동사>는 생략 가능하다.
She was willing to help others **though** *(she was)* very tired.
(그녀는 매우 피곤했지만 기꺼이 다른 사람들을 도왔다.)

다음 중 어법상 적절한 표현을 고르시오.

01   *Iggle-iggle* is an adverb that describes a fire burning, but it focuses on the heat rather than the shape of the flame, while / which *hwal-hwal* brings to mind flames that rise high up into the sky. [기출 응용]

02   Speaking in public is so difficult for people, especially businesspeople whose general style is that of understatement, which / that they should take an acting course before they take a speech course. [기출 응용]

03   After checking the accommodations, he came up to the purser's desk and inquired if / that he could leave his valuables in the ship's safe. [기출 응용]

04   Because of their communicative properties, the question is posed which / whether the arts should reflect society's standards or question them. [기출 응용]

05   Some of the water comes from underground sources and some from rain, and it is difficult to identify where / what the street tree is getting it. [기출 응용]

06   The lizards that climb walls and ceilings do not easily fall off. But it is not why / because they have great suction — as a matter of fact, they are not really using suction at all. [기출]

다음 밑줄 친 부분이 어법상 올바르면 ○표, 틀리면 ✕표하고 바르게 고치시오.

07   Those who donate to one or two charities seek evidence about what the charity is doing and <u>what</u> it is really having a positive impact. If the evidence indicates that the charity is really helping others, they make a substantial donation. [기출]

우리말에 맞도록 괄호 안의 어구를 바르게 배열하시오. (어형 변화 가능, 필요한 어구 추가 가능)

08   나는 그 국립공원에 입장하는 데 비용이 얼마나 드는지 궁금하다. (cost, how, the national park, enter)

I wonder _____.

Testing Point 11 전치사+명사(구), 접속사+절을 기억하라!

전체 기출 빈도 ◆◆◆◆◇
최근 기출 빈도 ◆◆◇◇◇

<예제> The dummy's job is to simulate a human being │ during / while │ a crash, collecting data that would not be possible to collect from a human occupant. [기출 응용]

출제의도 전치사와 접속사 자리 구분하기

해결전략 전치사 뒤에는 명사(구), 접속사 뒤에는 주어, 동사를 갖춘 절이 온다.

전치사+명사(구)	despite, in spite of (~에도 불구하고) / because of, owing to, due to, on account of (~ 때문에) / during (~ 동안에) / except (for), apart from (~을 제외하고) / such as (~와 같은) / in addition to (~ 외에 또)
접속사+절 (S+V ~)	although (비록 ~할지라도) / because, since (~하기 때문에) / while (~하는 동안에) / except (~하는 것을 제외하고)

다음 밑줄 친 부분의 구조에 주의하여 어법상 적절한 표현을 고르시오.

01 │ Because / Because of │ her interest in comets, she decided to study astronomy.

02 │ In spite of / Although │ she was in poor health, she continued to carry out her duties.

03 │ During / While │ the summer, she worked as a lifeguard at the beach.

04 │ Despite / Although │ our efforts to save the school, the authorities decided to close it.

05 I went to see the movie │ because / because of │ it had excellent reviews.

06 │ During / While │ he was asleep, thieves broke in.

전치사 / 접속사	as, since, until, before, after는 전치사와 접속사 모두로 쓰인다.

다음 밑줄 친 부분을 해석하시오.

07 You can use that glass **as** a vase.

08 Do this again **as** I told you this morning.

09 She's been my best friend **since** childhood.

10 The clock hasn't been working **since** the electricity was off.

11 **Since** the Earth is rotating, two tides occur every day.

Point Exercise

정답 및 해설 p. 28

다음 중 어법상 적절한 표현을 고르시오.

01 ┃ Although / Despite ┃ a person's good looks may get our attention, it is not an impression that necessarily lasts. [기출 응용]

02 Henry Curtis advises, "Make your plans as fantastic as you like ┃ because / because of ┃ twenty-five years from now, they will not seem so special." [기출 응용]

03 People suffering from SAD (seasonal affective disorder) become depressed ┃ while / during ┃ the winter months. Their depression appears to be a result of the reduction in the amount of sunlight they are exposed to. [기출 응용]

*seasonal affective disorder: 계절성 정서 장애(SAD)

04 Her father's business failed ┃ while / during ┃ Anita was in high school, so she quit school and found a job as a nurse's assistant in a hospital for homeless people. There, she became interested in social welfare. [기출 응용]

05 "I never gave up." These words have been voiced by mountain climbers who lay in freezing crevices until ┃ they / their ┃ rescue, and by people who have recovered from cancer, as well as by people who survived the Great Depression. [기출 응용] *the Great Depression: (1929년 미국에서 비롯된) 대공황

06 (A) ┃ Although / In spite of ┃ it being a latecomer, the company has grown remarkably since
도전 (B) ┃ it found / its foundation ┃, and finally has become the most profitable oil refiner in the country.

우리말에 맞도록 괄호 안의 어구를 바르게 배열하시오. (어형 변화 가능, 필요한 어구 추가 가능)

07 그 아이스크림 회사는 그 제품들이 어떤 이물질을 포함하고 있을지도 모르는 가능성 때문에 회사 제품들 중 일부를 자발적으로 회수하고 있다.

(the products, may, the possibility, contain, because, a foreign object)

The ice cream company is voluntarily recalling some of its products _____

_____ .

다음 중 어법상 적절한 표현을 고르시오.

01 Recently, a study found │that / what│ people who drank two glasses of water before meals got full sooner, ate fewer calories, and lost more weight. [기출]

02 Sometimes when you are supposed to be listening to someone, your mind starts to wander. All teachers know that this happens frequently with students in classes. It's what goes on inside your head that makes all the difference in how well you will convert │what / that│ you hear into something you learn. Listening is not enough. [기출]

다음 밑줄 친 부분이 어법상 올바르면 ○표, 틀리면 ×표하고 바르게 고치시오.

03 In early modern Europe, transport by water was usually much cheaper than transport by land. An Italian printer calculated in 1550 <u>that</u> to send a load of books from Rome to Lyons would cost 18 scudi by land compared with 4 by sea. [기출]   *scudi: 이탈리아의 옛 은화 단위(scudo)의 복수형

04 When it became clear to me <u>what</u> no doctor could answer my basic questions, I walked out of the hospital against medical advice. Returning to college, I pursued medicine with a great passion. [기출]

05 <u>What</u> some organisms must starve in nature is deeply regrettable and sad. The statement remains implacably true, even though starvation also may sometimes subserve ends that are good. [기출]   *implacably: 확고히   **subserve: 공헌하다

06 Compounding the difficulty, now more than ever, is <u>what</u> ergonomists call information overload, where a leader is overrun with inputs — via e-mails, meetings, and phone calls — that only distract and confuse her thinking. [기출 응용]   *ergonomist: 인간 공학자

07 Wikipedia was considered a joke when it started. Today it is so much more comprehensive than anything that came before it <u>that</u> it's widely considered the only encyclopedia. [기출 응용]

다음 밑줄 친 부분 중에서 어법상 틀린 곳을 찾아 기호를 쓰고 바르게 고치시오.

08 Behavioral economists — the economists who actually study (A) <u>that</u> people do as opposed to the kind who simply assume the human mind works like a calculator — have shown again and again (B) <u>that</u> people reject unfair offers even if it costs them money to do so. [기출 응용]

09 We have a deep intuition (A) <u>that</u> the future is open until it becomes present and (B) <u>what</u> the past is fixed. [기출 응용]

10 He concludes (A) <u>that</u> a decline of empathy and a rise in narcissism are exactly (B) <u>that</u> we would expect to see in children who have little opportunity to play socially. [기출 응용]

11 Are cats liquid or solid? That's the kind of question (A) <u>that</u> could win a scientist an Ig Nobel Prize, a parody of the Nobel Prize that honors research that "makes people laugh, then think." But it wasn't with this in mind (B) <u>what</u> Marc-Antoine Fardin, a physicist at Paris Diderot University, set out to find out whether house cats flow. [기출 응용]

12 It is impossible to guess from their bodies that birds make nests, and, sometimes, animals behave in a way quite contrary to (A) <u>that</u> might be expected from their physical form: ghost spiders have tremendously long legs, yet they weave webs out of very short threads. To a human observer, their legs seem a great hindrance (B) <u>as</u> they spin and move about the web.

[기출]

다음 빈칸에 들어갈 말을 쓰시오.

❶ 관계사 ▶ UNIT 03

- 관계사는 절과 절을 연결하는 1 _____ 역할을 하면서 관계사절 내에서 대명사/부사의 역할을 한다.
- 관계대명사의 격은 관계대명사가 관계대명사절에서 대신하는 문장 요소와 2 _____ 한다.
- 관계대명사 that, what은 계속적 용법으로 쓸 수 3 _____.
- 계속적 용법의 which: 단어뿐 아니라 어구, 절도 선행사로 할 수 있다.
- 관계부사절 내에서 관계부사는 '때, 장소, 이유, 방법'을 선행사로 하여 부사로 쓰인다.
- 4 _____ 에 적합한 관계부사가 왔는지 확인한다.
- how는 선행사 the way나 how 중 하나를 반드시 5 _____ 한다.
- 대명사나 부사는 절과 절을 연결할 수 없고 관계대명사나 관계부사와 중복해서 쓸 수도 없다.
- 주어 외에 동사가 필요로 하는 필수 요소인 목적어, 보어가 빠짐없이 갖춰져 있어야 완전한 절이다.
- 관계부사 뒤에는 6 _____ 구조, 관계대명사 뒤에는 7 _____ 구조가 온다.
- 복합관계대명사+8 _____ 구조: 문장에서 명사절이나 부사절을 이끈다.
- 복합관계부사+9 _____ 구조: 문장에서 부사절을 이끈다.

❷ 관계사, 접속사와 전치사 ▶ UNIT 04

- what과 that[which]은 뒤에 절이 완전한지 불완전한지와 앞에 선행사나 10 _____ 유무에 따라 판단한다.
- 11 _____ 뒤에는 명사(구), 12 _____ 뒤에는 주어, 동사를 갖춘 절이 온다.

다음 중 어법상 적절한 표현을 고르시오.

01 The growing field of genetics is showing us that / what many scientists have suspected for years — foods can immediately influence the genetic blueprint. [기출 응용]

02 Taking a bath in water whose temperature ranges between 35°C and 36°C helps calm you down when / what you are feeling nervous. [기출 응용]

03 As the villagers sat to eat, all eyes were on their noble guest. Everyone looked at what / how the man held his chopsticks, so that they could imitate him. [기출]

다음 밑줄 친 부분이 어법상 올바르면 ○표, 틀리면 ✕표하고 바르게 고치시오.

04 He was fond of saying that the biggest problem with managing computer programmers is that you can never tell <u>whether</u> they are working by looking at them. [기출 응용]

05 When asked to estimate how many calories <u>had they</u> eaten at the restaurants, people tended to underestimate the number of calories eaten at Olive Garden and to overestimate the number of calories eaten at McDonald's.

06 [도전] The audience, who had waited all their lives for this show, turned their eyes at the same time in the direction in <u>that</u> the singer was advancing.

07 When induced to give spoken or written witness to something they doubt, people will often feel bad about their deceit. Nevertheless, they begin to believe <u>that</u> they are saying. Without convincing evidence to the contrary, saying becomes believing. [기출 응용]

08 The two men were walking up a path toward Meredith's summerhouse, when Conan Doyle heard the old novelist fall behind him. He judged by the sound <u>which</u> the fall was a mere slip and could not have hurt Meredith. Therefore, he did not turn and he strode on as if he had heard nothing. [기출 응용]

09 At the most advanced levels, Double Dutch is being done as an extreme competition sport, <u>which</u> groups of kids are doing high-energy dance routines that are truly amazing. [기출 응용]

*Double Dutch: 두 개의 줄을 서로 반대쪽으로 돌리는 줄넘기 놀이

10 The brain still outclasses any desktop computer both in terms of the calculations it can perform and the efficiency <u>at which</u> it does this. [기출]

11 Alexander Fleming accidentally discovered a mold, penicillium notatum, <u>that</u> killed off bacteria in a petri dish. *petri dish: 페트리 접시(세균 배양 따위에 쓰이는, 둥글넓적한 작은 접시)

12   Some special effects are similar in principle to 3-D art, motion pictures, or visual illusions, none of <u>them</u> have been around long enough for our brains to have evolved special mechanisms to perceive them. [기출 응용]

13
도전
     What makes medical treatment overwhelming is not only that the medical decision is ours, but that the number of sources of information <u>which</u> we are to make the decisions has exploded. We now have encyclopedic lay-people's guides to health, "better health" magazines, and the Internet. [기출]   *lay-person: 비전문가 ((lay-people의 단수형))

14   Unfortunately, there's no way to know <u>whether</u> the memories hypnotized people retrieve are true or not—unless of course we know exactly what the person should be able to remember.

[기출]

15   Sound can travel through a variety of substances with different densities, and the physical characteristics of the medium through which the sound travels have a major influence on <u>how</u> the sound can be used. [기출]

16   Such primitive societies, <u>as</u> Steven Mithen emphasizes in *The Prehistory of the Modern Mind*, tend to view man and beast, animal and plant, organic and inorganic spheres, as participants in an integrated, animated totality. [기출]

17   Humans are so averse to feeling that they're being cheated <u>that</u> they often respond in ways that seemingly make little sense. [기출]   *averse to: ~을 싫어하는

18   Big university football coaches can earn more than $1 million a year. One degree higher up is the National Football League, <u>where</u> head coaches can earn many times more than their best-paid campus counterparts. [기출]

19   Children who visit their institutionalized parents or grandparents cannot help but remember <u>that</u> they once were and be depressed by their incapacities. [기출 응용]

20   Don't focus on the result itself. The reasoning here is <u>what</u> if you follow the steps required, then the result will look after itself. [기출 응용]

21   Baylor University researchers investigated <u>whether</u> different types of writing could ease people into sleep. [기출]

22   Ratios are much more important for survival in the wild than the ability to count. We needed to know instantly whether there were more adversaries than us. When we saw two trees we needed to know instantly <u>that</u> had more fruit hanging from it. [기출]

23   The most dramatic and significant contacts between civilizations were <u>when</u> people from one civilization conquered and eliminated the people of another. [기출]

24   If there's one thing koalas are good at, it's sleeping. For a long time many scientists suspected that koalas were so lethargic <u>because</u> the compounds in eucalyptus leaves kept the cute little animals in a drugged-out state. [기출]   *lethargic: 무기력한 **drugged-out: 몽롱한, 취한

다음 밑줄 친 부분 중 어법상 틀린 것을 찾아 기호를 쓰고 바르게 고치시오.

25   The first time I was told (A) <u>that</u> my face is very small was within a few days of arriving in Korea. It made me wonder (B) <u>if</u> there was something wrong with my face. I've since discovered that it's meant in praise, but at the time, I didn't know how (C) <u>should I</u> respond to it. [기출 응용]

PART
III

Usages

중요 형용사와 부사 ADJECTIVES & ADVERBS

Testing Point 12	형용사 자리인가, 부사 자리인가	전체 기출 빈도 ◆◆◆◆◆
		최근 기출 빈도 ◆◆◆◆◇

<예제> Psychologists have many theories about why people are so sensitive / sensitively to hearing about their own imperfections. [기출 응용]

출제의도 형용사 자리와 부사 자리 구분하기

해결전략 형용사는 명사 수식과 보어 역할을 한다. 부사는 명사 이외의 모든 품사 및 구, 절, 문장 전체를 수식하며
보어로는 쓰일 수 없다.

형용사	명사 앞이나 뒤에서 수식 / 보어 역할
부사	동사, 형용사, 부사, 혹은 구나 절, 문장 수식

• **<명사+형용사>**: 형용사 뒤에 <전치사+명사> 등의 수식어구가 뒤따라와서 길어지면 대개 명사 뒤에서 수식한다.
  a room full of flowers = a room (which is) full of flowers

다음 네모의 단어가 수식하는 부분에 밑줄을 긋고 어법상 적절한 표현을 고르시오.

01   The film was an immediate / immediately success.

02   I want to cook dishes which are enjoyable / enjoyably for all guests from every culture.

03   The team played brilliant / brilliantly in the first half.

04   In a labor-abundant country, wages tend to be relative / relatively low.

05   She left here exact / exactly at one o'clock.

06   Unfortunate / Unfortunately , his judgment was wrong.

다음 중 어법상 적절한 표현을 고르시오.

07   Many university students are, quite surprising / surprisingly , suffering from loneliness on campus.

08   My experience with your company has been terrible / terribly .

09   I made the climb easier / more easily by giving myself some time to rest.

형용사를 주격보어로 취하는 동사들	형용사를 목적격보어로 취하는 동사들
상태: be, remain, keep, stay 감각: look, smell, taste, sound, feel 등 인식: seem, appear 변화: become, get, grow, go, come, run, turn, fall	생각하다: think, believe, consider, find, feel ~하게 하다: make, drive, get ~한 상태로 두다: leave, keep, hold 등

구문 속 형용사 vs. 부사	형용사나 부사가 다 올 수 있는 곳은 문장 구조에 따라 적절한 것을 선택하면 된다.	
as ... as	10	Is the food as good / well as you expected?
	11	She speaks French as good / well as us.
the more ..., the more ~	12	The more physical / physically activity you do, the greater the health benefits.
	13	The more physical / physically active people were, the fewer depressive symptoms they reported.
how ~	14	I don't care how unfortunate / unfortunately she once was.
	15	Many people don't realize how severe / severely we have been affected by the problem.
so는 부사로서 부사와 형용사 모두 수식 가능	16	It's so easy / easily to get lost inside a problem that seems so big at the time.
	17	It's better to lead by doing because words are so easy / easily forgotten.

다음 중 어법상 적절한 표현을 고르시오.

❶ In neither case was it necessary / necessarily to find a guide for the trip.

❷ These are serious / seriously some of the best muffins I've ever had. They are so moist and flavorful.

❸ Our reason to offering this service is to make easy / easily the online business.

Guides

❶ 도치구문: (← It was **necessary** to find a guide for the trip.)
❷ <S+V+부사+C(명사 보어)>: 이때의 부사는 동사를 수식하는 것이다.
❸ <S+make+형용사 보어+목적어>: 5문형(SVOC) 동사인 make 뒤의 목적어가 명사구인 경우 보어 뒤에 위치시키는 경우가 있다 (SVCO). 주로 보어가 easy, (im)possible인 경우이다.

Point Exercise

정답 및 해설 p. 34

다음 중 어법상 적절한 표현을 고르시오.

01 Her concert was fantastic! The singing was great, the drumming was perfect and the rest of the instruments were played splendid / splendidly .

02 The remoras get a free ride through the water from the shark. He thought it would be interesting / interestingly to see the shark's life through the eyes of the remora. [기출 응용]

*remora: 빨판상어

03 You should pay close attention to someone's normal pattern in order to notice a deviation from it when he or she lies. Sometimes the variation is as subtle / subtly as a pause. [기출 응용]

04 도전 So desperate / desperately are we that we surrender to foolish ideas presented by others simply to show how open-minded we really are.

05 Good jugglers make juggling look so easy / easily that it is hard to imagine all the physics that comes into play. Gravity has a significant effect on each of the objects juggled. [기출 응용]

06 도전 Mourning a dead pet provides children with a useful "rehearsal" for the death of human family members, but it is not considered appropriate / appropriately for adults because there is a lack of social support for the mature person going through such grief. [기출 응용]

07 Mom was an (A) extraordinary / extraordinarily clean person. After feeding my brother and me breakfast, she would scrub, mop, and dust everything. As we grew older, Mom made sure we did our part by keeping our rooms (B) neat / neatly .

다음 밑줄 친 부분이 어법상 올바르면 ○표, 틀리면 ×표하고 바르게 고치시오.

08 When it comes to medical treatment, patients see choice as both a blessing and a burden. And the burden falls primarily on women, who are <u>typically</u> the guardians not only of their own health, but those of their husbands and children. [기출]

09 As you read a new word in context, there is a very good chance that you will be able to guess its meaning. Therefore, rather than working with word lists, it is <u>usual</u> best to see new words in context. [기출 응용]

10 At one time, many people thought the use of answering machines <u>rudely</u>. Today, the lack of an answering machine is considered inconsiderate since, without it, the caller cannot leave a message for a person who is away. [기출 응용]

11
도전

Starvation in nature helps filter out those less fit to survive and allow the emergence of a new species in place of the old one. Thus it is a disvalue that can help make <u>possible</u> the good of greater diversity. [기출 응용]

12 As a patient, and a teenager <u>eager</u> to return to college, I asked each doctor who examined me, "What caused my disease?" [기출]

다음 밑줄 친 부분 중에서 어법상 틀린 곳을 찾아 기호를 쓰고 바르게 고치시오.

13
도전

Make your plans ten times as (A) <u>greatly</u> as you first planned. If you push yourself to dream more (B) <u>expansively</u>, you will be forced to grow. And it will set you up to believe in greater possibilities. [기출 응용]

우리말에 맞도록 빈칸에 들어갈 어구를 <보기>에서 골라 바르게 변형하여 쓰시오.

<보기>   delicious, sweet, brilliant, fresh

14 사랑에 빠지면, 공기는 더 신선하게 느껴지고, 꽃은 더 향기로운 냄새가 나고, 음식은 더 맛있고, 밤하늘의 별도 더욱 반짝이며 빛난다.

When you fall in love, the air feels (A) _____ , the flowers smell (B) _____ , the food tastes (C) _____ , and the stars shine (D) _____ in the night sky.

형태가 비슷한 형용사, 부사 구별하기

전체 기출 빈도	◆◆◆◆◇
최근 기출 빈도	◆◆◇◇◇

<예제> If you try to make a short move on your own, you may find out too | late / lately | that your car cannot carry as much as you thought it could. [기출 응용]

출제의도 혼동되는 형용사와 부사 구별하기

해결전략 형태가 비슷한 형용사, 부사들은 형태별 의미와 쓰임을 알아두고 문맥을 고려하여 판단한다.

later (시간) 나중의; 나중에	latest (시간) (가장) 최근의[최신의]
latter (순서) (둘 중에서) 후자의; (나열된 것들 중) 마지막의	last (순서) 최후의; (시간상) 최종의; 지난 cf. the last 최근의, 최신의; 결코 ~할 것 같지 않은

01　Computers have always represented the **latest** in technology.

02　Turn left and after 50 meters we are the **last** house on the right.

late	형 늦은; 고인의 부 늦게	lately	부 최근에
near	형 가까운 부 가까이	nearly	부 거의
hard	형 단단한; 어려운 부 열심히; 세게	hardly	부 거의 ~않다
high	형 높은 부 높이	highly	부 아주, 매우
close	형 가까운; 면밀한 부 가까이	closely	부 면밀히; 밀접하게

03　Come | near / nearly | to me and listen to this.

04　This incident is | close / closely | connected to my job.

sleeping: 자는, 자고 있는 (명사 수식)	asleep: 잠이 든 (보어)
like: ~와 같이, ~처럼 (전치사)	alike: 서로 닮은 (보어) / 똑같이 (부사)
living: 살아 있는 (명사 수식) / 생활 (명사)	alive: 살아 있는 (보어)
lonely: 외로운 (명사 수식, 보어)	alone: 혼자; 외로운 (보어) / 혼자서, 혼자 힘으로 (부사)

05　Fire comes in many forms, | like / alike | candle flame, charcoal fire, and torch light. [기출]

06　The two pictures look exactly | like / alike |.

enough의 위치	enough 형 + 명사 형용사, 부사, 동사 + enough 부

07　I have **enough** *money* to pay the rent.

08　The room should be *large* **enough** to accommodate all people expected to attend.

Point Exercise

정답 및 해설 p. 35

다음 중 어법상 적절한 표현을 고르시오.

01 Maybe you thought you liked working lonely / alone , but now you're stuck in a tiny office with minimal human contact, realizing that you hate working in a secluded setting. [기출 응용]

02 It is surprising that a 24-hour study room is not available to students. Many students spend late nights working in the dark, trying not to wake sleeping / asleep roommates. There is no reason the university cannot provide an appropriate workspace for these students.

03 Our service is guaranteed to upgrade the quality of your living / alive environment. Call today to schedule your free in-home consultation. [기출 응용]

04 Each ball must be thrown enough high / high enough to allow the juggler time to handle the other balls. While throwing higher gives the juggler additional time, it also increases the risk of error. [기출 응용]

05 Falling in love is (A) like / alike being wrapped in a magical cloud. Your body feels (B) living / alive , and you jump out of bed each morning with a smile on your face. [기출 응용]

06 Editing the photographs you take is a big job, and one I have always hated. It is (A) hard / hardly to throw away something after you labor (B) hard / hardly to get it. You can (C) hard / hardly find it easy to discard the pictures, especially when they bring back good memories.

Testing Point 14   비교구문의 형태와 의미를 일치시켜라!

전체 기출 빈도 ◆◆◇◇◇
최근 기출 빈도 ◆◆◇◇◇

<예제> Building a legitimate market for digitally delivered music is far | much / more | complicated than most people have recognized.

출제의도 원급, 비교급, 최상급 표현 구분하기

해결전략 원급, 비교급, 최상급은 문맥상의 의미가 자연스러운지, 그리고 각각 짝을 이루는 구문의 나머지 표현이 무엇인지를 문장에서 확인한다.

원급	as 원급 as
비교급	비교급 than
최상급	the+최상급+of[in] 명사구 / the+최상급+관계사 that절

· **불규칙 변화 형용사/부사**

good[well]-better-best / bad[badly]/ill-worse-worst / many[much]-more-most / little-less-least

다음 중 어법상 적절한 표현을 고르시오.

01   His looks were as impressive | as / than | his personality.

02   The deer mouse has | large / larger | eyes and ears than those of the house mouse.

*deer mouse: 흰발생쥐

03   Playing baseball is | more / most | interesting than just watching games on TV.

04   Women are | less / least | likely to develop heart disease than men are.

05   I am | good / better | at English than at French.

06   The | more / most | memorable moment in the history of Korean soccer is the success of the 2002 World Cup.

07   *War and Peace* is the | longer / longest | book that I have ever read.

· **비교급, 부정주어, 원급 등을 이용한 최상급 의미 표현**

War and Peace is **longer than any other** book (that) I have ever read.
No (other) book (that) I have ever read is **longer than** *War and Peace*.
No (other) book (that) I have ever read is **as[so] long as** *War and Peace*.

Point Exercise

정답 및 해설 p. 36

다음 중 어법상 적절한 표현을 고르시오.

01   Most performers will have to play the mainstream repertory in order to secure some credibility. However, this repertory is not necessarily the same as the | most / best | repertory.

[기출 응용]

02   Holland scored a goal after ten minutes, and they were playing really well. After half time, however, England played | better / best |. Rooney, my favorite player, was excellent. [기출]

다음 밑줄 친 부분이 어법상 올바르면 ○표, 틀리면 ✕표하고 바르게 고치시오.

03   If the movie calls for rivers, mountains, or jungles, it may be cheaper to film in real places <u>as</u> to build imitation scenery. [기출 응용]

04   A board-certified pediatrician is the <u>more</u> knowledgeable of physicians when dealing with infant medical problems.   *board-certified: 전문의(醫)의, 전문 분야에서 인정을 받은

05   Like most parents, you might have spent money on a toy that your child didn't play with very much. You might have found your child playing <u>much</u> with the box than the toy that came in it. [기출 응용]

06   Creativity is strange in that it finds its way in any kind of situation, no matter how restricted, just as the same amount of water flows faster and stronger through a narrow strait <u>as</u> across the open sea. [기출]   *strait: 해협

비교급, 최상급을 수식하는 부사

> <예제> Robots can see, and in fact they can see [much / very] better than human beings, but they don't understand what they are seeing. [기출 응용]

출제의도 비교급과 원급 수식 부사 구분하기

해결전략 비교급을 수식하는 부사가 따로 있으며 very, more는 비교급을 수식할 수 없다.

비교급 수식 부사	much, even, (by) far, still, a lot, a great deal(훨씬), a little(약간), no(조금도 ~아닌) 등
최상급 수식 부사	(by) far, much, quite, the very 등

01   We need to get **much[far, even, still, a lot, a great deal]** *better* at allocating our marketing budget.

02   This is **by far** *the best* book about writing I have ever read!

• 문법책에서 흔히 제시되는 부사들 외에도 비교급을 수식할 수 있는 부사들은 많다. significantly(상당히), substantially(상당히), considerably(상당히), totally(완전히) 등 의미적으로 '정도'의 차이를 강조하는 데 자연스러운 것들이 이에 해당한다.

Point Exercise

정답 및 해설 p. 36

다음 중 어법상 적절한 표현을 고르시오.

01   Some toys floated along the Alaskan coast and across the Bering Sea. Other toys stayed at sea [even / very] longer. [기출 응용]

다음 밑줄 친 부분이 어법상 올바르면 ○표, 틀리면 ✕표하고 바르게 고치시오.

02   It can happen that one's memories grow <u>more</u> sharper even after a long passage of time.

[기출 응용]

03   Consider the University of Cambridge study which found that a group of eight-year-old children was able to identify <u>substantially</u> more characters from animations than common wildlife species. [기출]

UNIT Exercise

다음 중 어법상 적절한 표현을 고르시오.

01 School uniforms have their advantages. For example, they make all students feel (A) equal / equally to each other. Levels of income differ (B) great / greatly among families — some families are well-off, but many are not. School uniforms make all the students look the same regardless of their parents' financial status. [기출 응용]

다음 밑줄 친 부분이 어법상 올바르면 ○표, 틀리면 ×표하고 바르게 고치시오.

02 We may have built computers that can beat our top Grand Master chess players, but we are still far away from designing one that is capable of recognizing and picking up one of the chess pieces as <u>easy</u> as a typical three-year-old child can. [기출 응용]

03 Farmers plow soil to improve it for crops. However, this process removes the plant cover that holds soil particles in place, making soil <u>defenselessly</u> to wind and water erosion. [기출 응용]

04 Young people treat the mobile phone as an essential necessity of life and often prefer to use text messages to communicate with their friends. Young people also <u>increasingly</u> access social networking websites. [기출]

05 As a foreign student, you may encounter language problems in America. Spoken English may sound very (A) <u>rapidly</u>. You may have trouble understanding what a person says simply because he speaks so (B) <u>fast</u> that your comprehension cannot keep up. [기출 응용]

우리말에 맞도록 괄호 안의 어구를 바르게 배열하시오. (어형 변화 가능, 주어진 어구로만 배열할 것)

06 인간은 매우 감정적일 뿐만 아니라 그들은 온갖 종류의 편견에 영향을 받는다.
(humans, be, high, emotion)

Not only _____, but they are influenced by all sorts of biases.

명사와 대명사 NOUNS & PRONOUNS

Testing Point 16 대명사는 지시하는 대상의 성·수에 주의하고 올바른 격을 사용한다

전체 기출 빈도 ◆◆◆◆◆
최근 기출 빈도 ◆◆◆◆◇

<예제> There are those who take advantage of the television time to show off their talents, hoping to get that big chance that will carry | it / them | to stardom. [기출 응용]

출제의도 대명사가 가리키는 대상 파악하기

해결전략 대명사는 지시하는 대상의 성, 수에 주의하고 올바른 격을 사용해야 한다. 문장에서 가주어나 가목적어 역할을 하는지 살핀다.

성·수·격	대명사는 지시하는 대상과 성·수를 일치시키고 대명사의 위치에 따라 올바른 격을 사용해야 한다.

- <부사구[절]+주절> 구조에서 부사구[절]의 대명사가 주절의 명사를 대신할 수 있다.
  e.g. While **he** is no longer with us, **Wilson** remains one of my role models.
  (윌슨은 더는 우리 곁에 없지만, 그는 내 롤모델 중 한 명으로 남았다.)
- (의미상) 주어와 목적어가 같은 대상일 경우, 목적어는 재귀대명사를 쓴다.

다음 중 어법상 적절한 표현을 고르시오.

01 We can't give up electricity, but we can control the ways we use | it / them |. [기출]

02 Although | it / he | gave the mountain its name, George Everest was not the first man to explore it.

03 You don't have to be Shakespeare, but you do need to know how to express | you / yourself | properly in written form. [기출 응용]

대명사 it	대명사 it은 앞에 나온 단어 외에 구, 절을 대신하기도 한다. 진주어·진목적어를 대신해 가주어·가목적어 역할을 하기도 한다.

다음 밑줄 친 대명사 it이 대신하는 것을 문장에서 찾아 밑줄을 그으시오.

04 We hoped to go to Europe this year, but we had to put it off for a reason.

05 She is the best swimmer in our class, and she knows it well.

06 It is very important to help your child develop his or her self-confidence.

07 I consider it a great honor to have been chosen to receive this award.

| that vs. those | 앞에 나온 명사의 반복을 피하기 위해 that[those]을 쓴다. 이때 대신하는 명사의 수와 일치시킨다. |

· **<those who ~>: ~한 사람들**
Listen to the stories of **those who** went through such a hard time.
(그렇게 어려운 시간을 겪은 사람들의 이야기에 귀 기울여라.)

다음 네모 안의 대명사가 대신하는 것을 문장에서 찾아 밑줄을 긋고 어법상 적절한 표현을 고르시오.

08   The color of this furniture is brighter than | that / those | of my mom's.

09   Korean growth patterns resemble | that / those | of Western nations.

| it vs. one(s) | it이 특정 명사를 대신하여 '바로 그것'을 의미하는 반면, one은 불특정한 명사 '아무거나 하나'를 의미한다.
· one[ones]은 셀 수 없는 명사를 대신하여 쓰이지 못한다. |

다음 네모 안의 대명사가 대신하는 것을 문장에서 찾아 밑줄을 긋고 어법상 적절한 표현을 고르시오.

10   There is a great ice cream place around here and we should visit | it / one |.

11   If you think your smoke alarms are more than 10 years old, replace them with new | one / ones |.

Point Exercise

정답 및 해설 p. 38

다음 중 어법상 적절한 표현을 고르시오.

01   The mentally ill are faced with a unique set of challenges, and | its / their | interests will not be adequately represented if they have no right to vote. [기출 응용]

02   In some countries a coin with a hole is supposed to be lucky because it was long believed that a shell or stone with a hole in | them / it | could keep away evil spirits. [기출 응용]

03 Since the government banned the honking of car horns downtown, one taxi driver has changed his / him to a recording of a woman's voice saying, "Watch out!" [기출 응용]

04 Successful people are able to hold a conversation pretty well on almost any subject. If you want to be one of them, make it / them your mission to know what's going on in the world.

[기출 응용]

05 During the last several decades, Asia's glaciers have been melting at an alarming rate. According to Chinese researcher Yao Tandong, annual glacial runoff on the Tibetan Plateau and surrounding areas is roughly 20 percent more than that / those of 40 years ago. [기출 응용]

*runoff: 땅 위를 흐르는 물

06 When I arrived at my second job, a server immediately handed me my first order. "Make sure these hash browns are hot," she said, "because these people just left a restaurant down the street that kept serving them cold one / ones." [기출 응용]

*hash browns 해시 브라운즈(다진 감자와 양파를 섞어 노릇하게 지진 요리)

07 Many people think breakfast hurts their efforts to reduce calories, so they tend to skip their breakfast. But (A) it / they won't work well. In reality, weight-watchers who skip breakfast might stuff (B) them / themselves at lunch. [기출]

*weight-watcher: 체중 감량에 노력하는 사람

다음 밑줄 친 부분이 어법상 올바르면 ○표, 틀리면 ✕표하고 바르게 고치시오.

08
함정 Recently, a severe disease hit Asian countries hard, causing several hundred deaths. In spite of <u>their</u> close location to these countries, however, Korea has remained free of the deadly disease. [기출 응용]

09 The doctors used pioneering technology to cure Mr. Brown's heart disease. It did little harm to him and caused few complications although <u>its</u> cost much more than normal surgery.

10
도전 Picasso and Braque had a very strong cooperation, which resulted in the birth of cubism. They dressed alike in mechanics' clothes, and jokingly compared <u>them</u> to the Wright brothers. [기출 응용]

*cubism: 입체파, 큐비즘

11   By mistake, the guest dropped a slice of tofu onto his neighbor's lap. In order to save <u>himself</u> from any embarrassment, all the villagers at the banquet began to fling tofu into each other's laps. [기출 응용]

12   This workshop will demonstrate the implementation of the Faculty Development Program. Participants will learn about the benefits of this program and discuss how to adapt <u>them</u> for use in their own campuses. [기출 응용]

13   Our school believes it is important for undergraduates to learn the elements of critical reasoning and the scientific method before working on <u>its</u> research project.

14   Sometimes, the longer <u>that</u> takes for a work of art to reveal all of its subtleties to us, the more fond of that thing — whether it's music, art, dance, or architecture — we become. [기출]

다음 질문에 답하시오.

15   Most of us make at least three important decisions in our lives: where to live, what to do, and whom to do it with. 이런 선택을 하는 것은 성년기의 매우 자연스러운 부분이라서 (A) <u>그 선택들을 하는 최초의 인간들 중에 우리가 있다는 것을 잊어버리기 쉽다</u>. For most of recorded history, people lived where they were born, did what their parents had done, and associated with (B) <u>those</u> who were doing the same. [기출]

(1) 밑줄 친 (A)의 우리말에 맞도록 괄호 안의 어구를 모두 사용하여 바르게 배열하시오. (주어진 어구로만 배열할 것)

(we, it, are, that, to forget, among the first human beings, easy, is, to make, them)

Making these choices is such a natural part of adulthood that _____

_____ .

(2) 밑줄 친 (B) 부분이 어법상 올바르면 ○표, 틀리면 ✕표하고 바르게 고치시오.

명사의 기본은 '수'와 '수식어' 구별이다

<예제> At Cambridge he seems to have had few / little interest in other subjects except science and mathematics. [기출 응용]

출제의도 명사의 올바른 수식어 알기

해결전략 셀 수 있는 명사와 셀 수 없는 명사를 구별하고 수나 양을 나타내는 수식어를 구분해서 알아둔다.

셀 수 있는 명사	단수: a[an]+셀 수 있는 명사 복수: 셀 수 있는 명사+-s[es]
셀 수 없는 명사	단수·복수형이 따로 없으므로, 앞에 a[an]이 오거나 뒤에 -s[es]가 붙을 수 없다. advice / ignorance / money / violence / baggage, luggage / information / news / wealth / equipment / luck / scenery / evidence / stuff / furniture / machinery(기계(류)) / traffic, etc.

	셀 수 있는 명사	셀 수 없는 명사	공통
많은	many, a great[good, large] number of	much, a great[good, large] amount[deal] of	a lot[lots] of, plenty of
약간 있는	a few • only a few < a few < quite[not] a few 극히 소수의 < 약간의 < 상당수의	a little	some, any
거의 없는	few	little	
기타	both, a couple of, several, each, every		all, most, no

다음 중 어법상 적절한 표현을 고르시오.

01   These days a(n) number / amount of households are struggling with the burden of debt.

02   It can be tempting to purchase many / much cheap pieces of clothing, but a few / little quality items will save you money in the long run.

03   A large number / amount of education is required to raise the awareness of human rights.

04   This website didn't offer as many / much information as I needed, but there was a few / little information that I could refer to.

- **<every+숫자+복수명사>: ~마다** (정기적인 시간 간격)

There are buses into town **every *ten minutes***. (마을로 가는 버스가 십 분마다 있다.)

cf. 그 외 every가 쓰이는 표현

I will go skiing **every other day** during this winter vacation. (이틀에 한 번 = every second day)
(나는 이번 겨울 방학 동안 이틀에 한 번 스키를 타러 갈 것이다.)

I try to listen to the news on the radio **every hour on the hour**. (매시 정각에)
(나는 매시 정각에 라디오 뉴스를 들으려고 한다.)

many, much, **some, any**	막연한 수나 양의 사람, 사물, 수량을 나타내며 대명사나 형용사 둘 다 쓰인다. many는 수, much는 양을 뜻하며 some, any는 수와 양 모두 뜻할 수 있다.

05 Unfortunately, not **many** of ***the photographers*** were there.

06 How **much** of ***this book*** is fact and how **much** is fiction?

07 **Some** of ***her stories*** were quite funny.

08 I can't find **any** of ***my books*** on the table.

Point Exercise

정답 및 해설 p. 40

다음 중 어법상 적절한 표현을 고르시오.

01 In earlier times, people traded crops or objects they had made in exchange for the goods they needed. The first stores sold just a few / little products such as meat and bread. [기출 응용]

02 Knowing how to study can really save you some study time, and can help maximize the number / amount of material you can remember.

03 There are lots of myth / myths about taking care of bad breath. One of them is that mouthwash will make bad breath go away. Mouthwash only gets rid of it temporarily. [기출 응용]

*mouthwash: 구강 청결제

04 While the "time machine" game will not solve every / all your problems, it can give you an enormous amount of needed perspective. I find myself laughing at things that I used to take far too seriously. [기출 응용]

05 The sun shone straight down the street, and in a few / little minutes we felt very hot. [기출 응용]

06 To achieve market success, avoid a one-size-fits-all strategy that places too many / much emphasis on the "global" aspect alone. This means each country, community and individual has unique characteristics and needs. [기출 응용]

07 Remember what it was like to report on a daily deadline for the first time? Or to interview a city official for the first time? The journalism program at our college was a source of many / much of these firsts for you. [기출 응용]

08 India is an attractive place for investment for (A) several / a great deal of reasons. It is an emerging economy with (B) many / much potential for further growth and its cheap labor draws lots of multinational companies' manufacturing and call centers.

혼동하기 쉬운 대명사 구별하기

<예제> Mr. Potter was sailing on one of the greatest transatlantic ocean liners, but to his surprise, he found another / other passenger was to share the cabin with him.

출제의도 부정대명사의 쓰임 구분하기

해결전략 부정대명사[형용사]는 지시하거나 수식하는 명사의 수를 확인하고, 지시하는 것이 막연한 것인지 the가 붙은 특정 대상인지를 확인하며 판단한다.

one / another / the other	one / the other
● ● ●	● ●

다음 중 어법상 적절한 표현을 고르시오.

01 One of the problems is finding a school; another / the other is looking for a place to live in; and the other is buying furniture.

02 One end of the rope is tied to the anchor, while another / the other is tied to a big post.

some / others	some / others / the others
●● ●●● ●●	●● ●●● ●●

03 Some problems are easy to handle, but other / others might require a little help.

04 Some employees finished college, other / others completed graduate school, and the others received their doctoral degrees.

불특정한 대상: <another+단수명사> <other+복수명사>	특정 대상: <the other+단수[복수]명사>

05 Martin thought life would be much better if he were able to move to another / other city. [기출 응용]

06 You need other / others people to guide you in the right direction.

07 Your presentation will be graded by the other / others students in class.

08 The grass is always greener on the other / others side of the fence.

Point Exercise

정답 및 해설 p. 41

다음 중 어법상 적절한 표현을 고르시오.

01 These days, many products are very similar to one another in their quality and price. If the products are almost the same, what makes customers buy one brand instead of other / another ? [기출 응용]

02 When a lecturer presents a succession of new concepts, students' faces begin to show signs of anguish and frustration; some write furiously in their notebooks, while other / others give up writing in complete discouragement. [기출 응용]

03 Shortly after the lifeguard managed to reach one of the two boys and pick him up on his surfboard, he dived into the chilly water seven times, looking for the other / another , but had no luck. [기출 응용]

04 도전 The summer Olympic Games contain some events with misleading names. For instance, the triple jump does not include three jumps but is made up of a hop, a skip, and a jump. The other / Another event is the hammer throw. The hammer does not look like a carpenter's tool at all. It is a metal ball on a chain. [기출 응용]

05 When elephants see that a predator is about to attack, they use their trunks to make a loud trumpet-like sound. This warns other / another elephants in the herd of possible danger.

[기출 응용]

다음 중 어법상 적절한 표현을 고르시오.

01 Sadly, human beings are in fact the only species that will deliberately deprive them / themselves of sleep without legitimate gain. [기출]

02 When you learn a new word it takes several repetitions at various intervals for the word to be mastered. To recall the word later you will need to activate "synapses" until eventually you know the word without consciously thinking about it / them . [기출 응용]

다음 밑줄 친 부분이 어법상 올바르면 ○표, 틀리면 ×표하고 바르게 고치시오.

03 Looking up at the stars in the night sky, it's quite obvious that they aren't all the same; some of them shine outstandingly brightly, while <u>others</u> are so faint that you cannot see them directly and can only see them with a telescope.

04 It is interesting that the ability to think about why things happen is one of the key abilities that separates human abilities from <u>those</u> of just about every other animal on the planet. [기출]

05 With <u>its</u> electrical and mechanical system, the washing machine is one of the most technologically advanced examples of a large household appliance. [기출]

06 White flour has <u>few</u> nutritional value due to the loss of most of the vitamins originally present in wheat, and it has low fiber content, which causes digestive problems.

07 Like that area in the side mirror of your car where you can't see that truck in the lane next to you, personal blind spots can easily be overlooked because you are completely unaware of <u>their</u> presence. [기출 응용]

UNIT 07 중요 동사 VERBS

Testing Point 19 · 동사에 따른 목적격보어의 형태에 주의하라!

전체 기출 빈도 ◆◆◆◆◇
최근 기출 빈도 ◆◆◇◇◇

<예제>

1. A movie set is built "on location," which means outside the studio. This enables the film makers │use / to use│ actual physical landscape as the scenery. [기출 응용]

2. Driving home with my family one day, I noticed smoke │risen / rising│ from the roof of an apartment building. [기출 응용]

출제의도 목적격보어로 쓰인 준동사 형태 알기

해결전략 목적격보어는 동사에 따라 취하는 형태가 다르며, 목적어와 목적격보어의 능동, 수동 의미 관계를 확인해야 한다.

동사+목적어+to-v	ask, tell, need, warn, expect, remind, invite, order, require, advise, persuade, convince, allow, permit, enable, get, cause, force, urge, encourage, want, tempt: (목적어)가 v하기를[v하도록] ~하다
동사+목적어+v	사역동사(make, have, let): (목적어)가 v하게 하다[시키다] 지각동사(feel, hear, listen to, see, watch, look at, notice, observe): (목적어)가 v하는 것을 ~하다
동사+목적어+v-ing	지각동사: (목적어)가 v하고 있는 것을 ~하다
동사+목적어+p.p.	make, get: (목적어)가 v되도록 하다 have: (남을 시켜) (목적어)가 v되도록 하다; (목적어)가 v되는 것을 당하다 keep, leave: (목적어)가 v된 채로 두다 find, feel, see, hear: (목적어)가 v된[되는] 것을 ~하다 like: (목적어)가 v된 것을 좋아하다 need: (목적어)가 v될 필요가 있다 want: (목적어)가 v되는 것을 원하다

• <help+목적어+(to-)v>: (목적어)가 v하는 것을 돕다

다음 괄호 안에 주어진 단어를 올바른 형태로 바꿔 쓰시오.

01   The reporter asked her (answer) _____ questions about her future plan.

02   I heard this song (play) _____ for the first time at a concert.

03   He heard her (play) _____ the violin at midnight.

04   She wanted her paintings (display) _____ in the gallery.

05   Lots of schools required students (read) _____ newspapers every day.

06   We strongly advise you not (bring) _____ any valuable items to the gym.

07   He felt himself (touch) _____ on his shoulder.

08   Stores usually allow customers (return) _____ merchandise.

09   I felt the water temperature (change) _____ dramatically.

10   The poor harvest caused prices (rise) _____ sharply.

11   We want our children (be) _____ competitive.

12   This drink made their pains and fever (go away) _____ . [기출 응용]

13   You need the program to have lost files (recover) _____ . [기출 응용]

14   We saw the tightrope walker (fall) _____ off the rope.

15   She almost had to shout to make herself (hear) _____ above the noise.

16   They returned after the storm and found their house (destroy) _____ .

다음 중 어법상 적절한 표현을 고르시오.

❶   I watched a man on the Métro, the subway in Paris, try / tried to get off the train and fail. He must not have known the doors don't open automatically at each station. [기출 응용]

❷   Timothy Lawson explored the spotlight effect by having college students change / changed into a sweatshirt with a big popular logo on the front before meeting a group of peers. [기출]

Guides

❶   목적어와 목적격보어 사이에 각각의 수식어(구)나 삽입어(구) 등이 더해져 서로 많이 떨어져 있을 수 있다. 특히 목적격보어 자리를 동사 자리로 착각하지 않도록 주의하자.

❷   동사별로 가능한 목적격보어의 형태와 그 의미를 정확하게 구별해서 알아두고 문맥을 잘 파악하여 적용해야 한다.

Point Exercise

정답 및 해설 p. 43

다음 중 어법상 적절한 표현을 고르시오.

01 People are using all kinds of methods to make themselves to appear / appear more attractive, at least on the outside. [기출 응용]

02 In a survey published earlier this year, seven out of ten parents said they would never let their children play / to play with toy guns. [기출 응용]

03 Severe weather is always a possibility anywhere on the globe, but we never really expect our own area to be / being affected. [기출 응용]

04 Examine your thoughts, and you will find them totally to occupy / occupied with the past or the future. [기출 응용]

05 The right side of the face is usually more relaxed and smoother than the left side. That is why movie stars prefer to have the right side of their face photograph / photographed . [기출 응용]

06 Our basic nature is to act, and not to be acted upon. Not only does this enable us (A) choose / to choose our response to particular circumstances, but this encourages us (B) to create / creating circumstances. [기출 응용]

07 Keep your radio (A) tuning / tuned to a weather station, as it will keep you (B) advising / advised of the storm's path.

다음 밑줄 친 부분이 어법상 올바르면 ○표, 틀리면 ✕표하고 바르게 고치시오.

08 If you were to step in quicksand, the weight of your body would cause the sand <u>acting</u> more like a liquid, and you'd sink right in. [기출 응용]   *quicksand: 표사(올라서면 빠져버리는 젖은 모래층)

09 The knowledge of another's personal affairs can tempt the possessor of this information <u>to repeat</u> it as gossip because as unrevealed information it remains socially inactive. [기출]

10
도전
A bamboo blind is generally used in summer for the circulation of air. It helps to keep rooms cool and <u>shading</u>, and makes the interior of a room almost invisible from the outside. [기출 응용]

11 We can't overstate the importance of the calendar tool in helping kids feel in control of their day. Have them <u>cross</u> off days of the week as you come to them.

12 When I saw him (A) <u>being interviewed</u> on television some months later, and heard him (B) <u>declared</u> that his only interest in life was playing bridge, to my great disappointment he was transformed before my eyes into an astoundingly unappealing man. [기출 응용]

우리말에 맞도록 괄호 안의 어구를 바르게 배열하시오. (어형 변화 가능, 주어진 어구로만 배열할 것)

13 사고 후에 차를 수리시키는 것에 관한 한 가장 중요한 점은 처음에 제대로 되도록 시키는 것이다.

(the first time, have, have, be, your car, do, after an accident, it, repair, right)

The most important thing when it comes to _____

_____ .

Testing Point 20　do 동사의 여러 쓰임

전체 기출 빈도　◆◆◆◇◇
최근 기출 빈도　◆◆◆◇◇

> <예제> Looking back, I learned more from my failures than I │ was / did │ from my successes. [기출 응용]

출제의도 do의 쓰임 파악하기

해결전략 do/does/did는 앞에 쓰인 일반동사를 대신하여 쓰이거나 동사를 강조할 때, 그리고 도치구문에서 쓰일 수 있다.

대동사	일반동사 이하의 반복을 피하기 위해 do[does/did]를 사용한다. 대동사의 주어가 되는 것의 수와 인칭, 그리고 시제에 주의하여 선택한다. 단, 앞 절이 <be동사+보어>이고 이를 대신할 때는 be동사를 사용하고, 앞 절에 쓰인 수동태를 대신할 때에도 be동사를 사용한다.

다음 중 어법상 적절한 표현을 고르시오.

01 Many people probably spend more time on the Internet than they │ do / did │ in their cars.

02 She plays tennis better now than she │ does / did │ last month.

03 Taking photos is more popular today than it │ was / did │ in the past.

04 In the UK, milk is generally not a good source of vitamin D because it is not fortified, as it │ is / does │ in some other countries.
*fortify: (음식에 영양소를) 첨가[강화]하다

강조, 도치	동사를 강조하거나 주어, 동사가 도치될 때 사용한다.

05 Germans **do** like to discuss things a lot.

06 Not only **does** God play dice, but he sometimes throws them where they cannot be seen.
- Stephen Hawking

• <than[as]+대동사+주어>: 주어가 대명사가 아닌 경우, 도치되는 경우가 많다.
　The Soviets tended to fight more effectively in winter than **did** *the Germans*.
　(소련은 독일군보다 겨울에 더 효과적으로 싸우는 경향이 있었다.)
　Our readers were not as serious as **were** *the readers* of the competitive magazine.
　(우리 독자들은 경쟁 잡지의 독자만큼 진지하지 않았다.)

Point Exercise

정답 및 해설 p. 44

다음 중 어법상 적절한 표현을 고르시오.

01 There are some women who feel the same parental love for other children as they do / are for their own. [기출 응용]

02 As civilizations developed, so were / did fashions. Body decoration, however, was, and still is the most popular means of showing human vanity. [기출 응용]

03 We do not hear with our eyes, but sometimes it almost seems as if we are / do . [기출 응용]

다음 밑줄 친 부분이 어법상 올바르면 ○표, 틀리면 ✕표하고 바르게 고치시오.

04
도전
"Monumental" is a word that comes very close to expressing the basic characteristic of Egyptian art. Never before and never since has the quality of monumentality been achieved as fully as it did in Egypt. [기출] *monumentality: 기념비적임, 장대하고 장엄함

05 Those who give small amounts to many charities are not so interested in whether what they are doing helps others — psychologists call them warm glow givers. [기출]

우리말에 맞도록 괄호 안의 어구를 바르게 배열하시오. (주어진 어구로만 배열할 것)

06 감사하는 마음을 갖는 사람들은 훌륭한 결정을 내리는 경향이 있다. 이기적인 어른들이나 아이들은 감사하는 마음을 갖는 사람들이 하는 것만큼 건전한 결정을 내리지 못한다.

(as well as, make, do, grateful people, sound decisions)

Grateful people are inclined to make healthy decisions. Selfish adults or kids do not

_____ .

혼동하기 쉬운 동사들을 정리하라!

전체 기출 빈도 ◆◆◇◇◇
최근 기출 빈도 ◆◇◇◇◇

<예제> Many of the world's major cities still lie / lay on the banks of rivers. [기출 응용]

출제의도 동사 변화형 구분하기

해결전략 목적어 유무로 자동사나 타동사를 구분하고 시제와 문맥도 확인한다.

lie vs. lay	lie(-lied-lied) / lying	짜 거짓말하다
	lie(-lay-lain) / lying	짜 놓여 있다; 누워 있다; ~인 채로 있다
	lay(-laid-laid) / laying	타 ~을 놓다(=put); ~을 눕히다
rise vs. raise	rise(-rose-risen)	짜 일어서다, 솟아오르다
	raise(-raised-raised)	타 ~을 올리다; (문제 등을) 제기하다
arise vs. arouse	arise(-arose-arisen)	짜 발생하다
	arouse(-aroused-aroused)	타 ~을 불러일으키다
fall vs. fell	fall(-fell-fallen)	짜 떨어지다, 내리다
	fell(-felled-felled)	타 ~을 쓰러뜨리다
find vs. found	find(-found-found)	타 ~을 찾다, 발견하다
	found(-founded-founded)	타 ~을 설립하다(=establish)
wind vs. wound.	wind[waind](-wound[waund]-wound)	짜 굽어지다 타 ~을 감다
	wound[wuːnd](-wounded-wounded)	타 ~에 상처를 입히다

다음 중 어법상 적절한 표현을 고르시오.

01 He lied / laid his hand on my shoulder.

02 Statistics can often lie / lay . We need to see details on these results.

03 She lay / laid back against the pillows.

04 The difficulty lays / lies in providing enough evidence.

05 She picked up her bag and raised / rose to leave.

06 Raise / Rise your hand if you know the right answer.

07 Several important legal questions arouse / arose in the contract negotiations.

08 Betty rose / raised the important question of who would be in charge.

09 Matt's behavior was arousing / arising the interest of the neighbors.

10 More than 100 trees were fell / felled by the great storm in just an hour.

11 The number of subscribers has fallen / fell to 1,000.

12 He tried to open the door and found / founded it unlocked.

13 Found / Founded in 1935 in Ohio, the organization is now worldwide.

14 The path winds / wounds along the riverside.

15 The doctor wound / wounded the bandage around his arm.

16 How many US soldiers were wound / wounded in the war?

Point Exercise

정답 및 해설 p. 45

다음 중 어법상 적절한 표현을 고르시오.

01 Some psychologists think that the origin of jealousy lies / lays in biology; in other words, that jealousy is an instinctive response in humans. [기출 응용]

02 Sometimes things change without appearing to change at all. Let's take a stone lying / laying on a beach as an example. During the day the stone is heated by the sun's rays. At night it cools down. [기출 응용]

03 Families in ancient Egypt mourned the death of a pet cat and had its body wrapped in cloth
도전 before it was finally laid / lain to rest. [기출 응용]

04 By the time she was three, Matilda had taught herself to read by studying newspapers and magazines that lay / laid around the house. At the age of four, she could read fast and well.
[기출 응용]

05 A few institutions of higher education have been laying / lying the groundwork for the online learning environment since the early 1990s.

06 Never give up hope, however frightening the obstacles lying / laying in your path are. [기출 응용]

07 She asked me several times to show her where I was (A) wound / wounded , so I unwrapped
도전 the gauze that was (B) wound / wounded around my chest.

최다 기출 동사, 중요 동사 정리

CASE 1 WANT, WISH, HOPE, EXPECT

아래의 네 동사들은 서로 비슷한 뜻을 가지고 있지만 동사 뒤의 구조가 조금씩 다르므로 유의해야 한다.

1. want

want+명사(구)	A recent survey has found that shoppers **want** *more time* for themselves in stores. [기출 응용]
want+to-v	I **want** *to submit* my new application by the end of June. [기출 응용]
want+O+OC	I didn't know my mother **wanted** *the laundry **done*** today.

2. wish

wish+for 명사(구)	She **wished** *for peace* with her whole heart.
wish(+O)+to-v	He was not sure whether he **wished** *her to stay* longer.
wish+IO+DO	I **wish** *you **all the happiness and joy*** that life can bring. [기출 응용]
wish+(that) S+V	I **wish** *that Kathy could hear this cheer, too*. [기출 응용] wish가 that절을 목적어로 취할 때 that절 내의 동사는 가정법 형태임에 주의.

3. hope

hope+for 명사(구)	We **are hoping** *for good weather* on Sunday.
hope+to-v	She can't read but **hopes** *to learn* to read. [기출 응용]
hope+(that) S+V	I **hope** *that you will pass the exam*.

4. expect

expect+명사(구)	Experts say that the average worker can **expect** *a pay increase of about 5%* in 2009.
expect+to-v	We can hardly **expect** *to learn* without making a good many mistakes in the learning process. [기출 응용]
expect+O+to-v	We can't **expect** *everyone to ride* a bike to work or school. [기출 응용] *He **was** once **expected** to be a good painter*. [기출 응용]
expect+(that) S+V	**Expecting** *that a blanket will always make something warm*, they think that it must warm ice, too. But its main role is to prevent heat loss. [기출 응용]

CASE 2 NEED, WANT, DESERVE

이 동사들은 뒤에 to be p.p.가 올 경우 v-ing로 대체 가능하다.
1. That boy's face **needs** *to be washed*.
   = That boy's face **needs** *washing*.
2. The windows **wanted** *to be cleaned*.
   = The windows **wanted** *cleaning*.
3. He **deserves** *to be locked up* for what he did.
   = He **deserves** *locking up* for what he did.

CASE 3 It takes+{시간, 노력, 돈, …}+(for 목적격)+to-v

'(누가) ~하는 데 얼마의 {시간, 노력, 돈, …}이 든다'라고 해석한다.
1. **It takes** *two incomes* **for** a family **to enjoy** more than just the basics.
2. The traffic is so bad that **it** can **take** *hours* **to drive** a short distance. [기출 응용]
cf. **S + spend + {시간, 노력, 돈, …} + (in) v-ing**

   As a consultant, I was supposed to **spend** *an hour or more* with the department heads **discussing** their thoughts. [기출 응용]

확인학습

정답 및 해설 p. 46

다음 중 어법상 적절한 표현을 고르시오.

01   My children want / wish it could be Christmas every day.

02   I hope his new film to go / will go smoothly and be welcomed by audiences.

03   Anybody can be an idiot, but it takes many hours of practice making / to make our idiocy funny. [기출 응용]

04   Korea is expected become / to become an aged society by 2018, when the proportion of citizens aged 65 or over will reach 14.4 percent.

다음 중 어법상 적절한 표현을 고르시오.

01 Salad vegetables like lettuce, cucumbers, and tomatoes have a very high water content, as [are / do] broth-based soups. [기출]

02 Plan ahead to prevent the grass from drying out — don't have a new lawn [lay / laid] if you are going on holiday, or if you are going to be away for some time as watering needs to be carried out every day.

03 If you're planning to sell your house, it's never a bad idea to get your carpet (A) [to clean / cleaned]. A carpet that looks well maintained can make your home (B) [look / to look] better and will be much more appealing to prospective buyers.

다음 밑줄 친 부분이 어법상 올바르면 ○표, 틀리면 ✕표하고 바르게 고치시오.

04 I slowed and allowed her to turn in front of me. I was feeling pretty good until, a couple of blocks later, she stopped to let a few more cars into the line, causing us both to miss the next light. I found myself completely <u>irritated</u> with her. [기출]

05 The washing machine not only cleans clothes, but it <u>is</u> so with far less water, detergent, and energy than washing by hand requires. [기출]

06 Productivity improvements are as important to the economy as they <u>do</u> to the individual business that's making them. [기출]

07 I had him <u>identified</u> his mistakes so that he can fix his own errors on his final tomorrow. We also discussed test taking strategies as well.

08 The play, *A Midsummer Night's Dream*, was written for Queen Elizabeth I, who may have had the play <u>perform</u> for her privately but she also frequented the playhouses to see performances.

09 People under hypnosis generate more "memories" than they <u>do</u> in a normal state, but these recollections are as likely to be false as true. [기출]   *hypnosis: 최면

10 If a certain method of learning a foreign language doesn't work for you, you should keep trying until you find the one which will both keep you <u>motivating</u> and get you the wanted results.

다음 빈칸에 들어갈 단어를 <보기>에서 골라 바르게 변형하여 쓰시오.

<보기> be, do, few, little

11 Cutting calories appears to promote weight loss more effectively than (A) _____ increasing exercise. The key to weight loss is to consume (B) _____ calories than you burn. For most people, it's generally easier to lower calorie intake than it (C) _____ to burn enough calories through exercise.

다음 밑줄 친 부분 중 어법상 <u>틀린</u> 것을 찾아 기호를 쓰고 바르게 고치시오.

12 Dark grey clouds (A) <u>lie</u> thick and heavy over Edmonton. Weather like this used to put a smile on my face, as it meant that snow was about to (B) <u>fall</u>, and I knew that whenever snow fell, the temperature usually (C) <u>raised</u>, and the sounds of the city were softened, as though one was hearing them through thick layers of cotton. [기출 응용]

다음 빈칸에 들어갈 말을 쓰시오.

❶ **중요 형용사와 부사** ▶ UNIT 05

- 형용사는 명사 수식과 보어 역할을 한다. 부사는 1 _____ 이외의 모든 품사 및 구, 절, 문장 전체를 수식하며
  2 _____로는 쓰일 수 없다.
- 형용사나 부사를 모두 쓸 수 있는 경우, 문장 구조에 따라 적절한 것을 선택하면 된다.
- 형태가 비슷한 형용사, 부사들은 형태별 의미와 쓰임을 알아두고 3 _____ 을 고려하여 판단한다.
- 원급, 비교급, 최상급은 문맥상의 의미가 자연스러운지, 그리고 각각 짝을 이루는 구문의 나머지 표현이 무엇인지를 문장에서
  확인한다.
- 비교급을 수식하는 부사가 따로 있으며 very, more는 4 _____ 을 수식할 수 없다.

❷ **명사와 대명사** ▶ UNIT 06

- 대명사는 지시하는 명사에 성, 수를 일치시키고 대명사의 위치에 따라 올바른 격을 사용해야 한다. 종속절의 명사는 주절의
  동일한 명사를 대명사로 바꿀 수 있다. 주어와 목적어가 같은 대상일 경우, 목적어는 5 _____를 쓴다.
- 대명사 6 _____은 앞에 나온 단어 외에 구, 절을 대신하기도 한다. 진주어·진목적어를 대신해 가주어·가목적어 역할을
  하기도 한다.
- 앞에 나온 명사의 반복을 피하기 위해 that[those]을 쓰는데 이때 대신하는 명사의 수와 일치시켜야 한다.
- it이 특정 명사를 대신하여 '바로 그것'을 의미하는 반면, 7 _____은 불특정한 명사 '아무거나 하나'를 의미한다. 참고로,
  one[ones]는 8 _____를 대신하여 쓰이지 못한다.
- 셀 수 있는 명사와 셀 수 없는 명사를 구별하고 수나 양을 나타내는 수식어를 구분해서 알아둔다.
- many, much, some, any 등은 막연한 수나 양의 사람, 사물, 수량을 나타내며 대명사나 형용사 둘 다 쓰인다.
- one, another, others 등의 부정대명사[형용사]는 지시하거나 수식하는 명사의 9 _____를 확인하고, 지시하는 것이
  막연한 것인지 10 _____가 붙은 특정 대상인지 확인한다.

❸ **중요 동사** ▶ UNIT 07

- 목적격보어는 동사에 따라 취하는 목적격보어의 형태가 다르며 11 _____와 목적격보어의 능동, 수동 의미 관계를 확인
  해야 한다.
- do/does/did는 앞에 쓰인 12 _____를 대신하여 쓰이거나 동사를 강조할 때, 그리고 도치구문에서 쓰일 수 있다.
- 혼동하기 쉬운 동사들은 목적어 유무로 자동사나 타동사를 구분하고 13 _____와 14 _____도 확인한다.

정답 및 해설 p. 47

다음 중 어법상 적절한 표현을 고르시오.

01   Argentina is a country located at the southern tip of South America. To the north lay / lie
Bolivia, Paraguay, and Uruguay; to the west is Chile. [기출 응용]

02   Depression really does change the way you see the world. People with the condition find it
easy / easily to interpret large images or scenes, but struggle to "spot the difference" in fine
detail. [기출]

03   One might say, "I'm not very successful in business because I'm the youngest child and thus
less aggressively / aggressive than my older brothers and sisters." Recent studies, however,
have proved this belief to be false. [기출]

04   To prevent an environmental crisis, South Korea is getting serious about recycling. It
(A) was found / was founded that over 30% of the garbage around Korean cities was from
fast-food chains. So the government launched a campaign to get fast-food restaurants
(B) recycle / to recycle 90% of their waste. [기출 응용]

다음 밑줄 친 부분이 어법상 올바르면 ○표, 틀리면 ✕표하고 바르게 고치시오.

05
도전   Evaluation of performances such as diving, gymnastics, and figure skating is somewhat
subjective — although elaborate scoring rules help make <u>them</u> more objective. [기출]

06   If you have to eat or drink something unpleasant, the best way is to hold your nose until
you've swallowed. <u>Other</u> way is to chew quickly and swallow quickly. [기출 응용]

07   Some people lived in an apartment building close to a busy state highway. They were made
<u>miserably</u> by the noise, and they complained to the city government. [기출 응용]

08
도전

Suppose, on your wedding day, your best man delivers a moving toast. You later learn he bought it online. Then, would the toast mean less than it was at first, before you knew it was written by a paid professional? [기출 응용]

09

Children at play often take on other roles, pretending to be Principal Walsh or Josh's mom, happily forcing themselves to imagine how someone else thinks and feels. [기출]

10

The modern adult human brain weighs only 1/50 of the total body weight but uses up to 1/5 of the total energy needs. The brain's running costs are about eight to ten times as high, per unit mass, as that of the body's muscles. [기출]

11

The Greeks fought each other and traded with each other far more often than they did with Persians or other non-Greeks. [기출]

12

Those who give small amounts to many charities are not so interested in whether what they are doing helps others. Knowing that they are giving makes themselves feel good, regardless of the impact of their donation. [기출 응용]

13

A recent study has found that the brains of children addicted to social media and video games are similar to that of drug or alcohol addicts.

14

The famous lecturer announced he had been diagnosed with Parkinson's disease after the audience noticed his hands shaking during a public lecture.

15 Pollen, which is one of <u>the more</u> common causes of allergies, is a powdery substance produced by trees, flowers, grasses, and weeds, and it is moved from the male components of a plant to the female parts.

16 Although the Alaskan residential market is <u>relative</u> small when compared to other states within the continental United States, its lack of size does not mean it has decreased activity.

17 Taiwan-born film director Ang Lee remembered his first days of filming in Britain were difficult. While he was used to making all the decisions and having them (A) <u>carry</u> out promptly, Ang Lee found that the British film-making style allowed everyone (B) <u>have</u> an opinion. [기출 응용]

다음 밑줄 친 부분 중 어법상 **틀린** 것을 찾아 기호를 쓰고 바르게 고치시오.

18 We have a deep intuition that the future is open until it becomes (A) <u>present</u> and that the past is fixed. As time flows, this structure of fixed past, immediate present and open future gets carried forward in time. Yet as (B) <u>naturally</u> as this way of thinking is, you will not find it (C) <u>reflected</u> in science. The equations of physics do not tell us which events are occurring right now — they are like a map without the "you are here" symbol. [기출 응용]

PART
IV

How to Use Verbs

UNIT 08 일치 AGREEMENT

Testing Point 22 수식어구와 진짜 주어를 혼동하지 마라!

전체 기출 빈도 ♦♦♦♦♦
최근 기출 빈도 ♦♦♦♦♦

<예제> The only difference between grapes and raisins [is / are] that grapes have about 6 times as much water in them. [기출]

출제의도 주어와 주어의 수식어구[절] 구분하기

해결전략 동사 바로 앞에 나온 주어의 수식어구를 주어로 혼동하지 말아야 한다.

주어+수식어구	주어+전명구 ~	주어+p.p. ~
	주어+v-ing ~	주어+형용사구 ~
	주어+to-v ~	

• 수식어구들은 여러 개가 겹쳐서 올 수도 있다.

다음 문장에서 주어를 찾아 밑줄을 긋고 어법상 적절한 표현을 고르시오.

01 All information available on our web pages [fall / falls] under copyright act.

02 A person with a special knowledge or ability [are / is] called an expert.

03 The files attached to the e-mail [seem / seems] to be infected with a virus.

04 His hand holding the wine glass [was / were] trembling and the wine spilled.

05 Deficient parts to be replaced [are / is] marked with special tags.

주어+수식어절	주어+관계사절 ~
	주어+동격절 ~

06 The rumor that the company would shut down [has / have] been proved false.

07 A battery that has not been used for several months [need / needs] to be charged for at least 14 hours before use.

• 수식어구와 삽입어구가 동시에 올 수도 있다.

08   Heart disease caused by fatty buildup in the blood vessels, which is very common in the general population, are / is even more common in people with certain diseases.

09   This blue hole, located in the southern Berry Islands, are / is about 600 feet wide.

Point Exercise

정답 및 해설 p. 49

다음 중 어법상 적절한 표현을 고르시오.

01   The election will be fair only if people capable of voting is / are also able to monitor the vote.

02   People of Northern Burma, who think in the Jinghpaw language, has / have eighteen basic terms for describing their kin. [기출]

03   Sleep deprivation has a great influence on the immune system. The main reason for these minor but unpleasant illnesses are / is that we are exhausted. We are all sleep-deprived from constant stress and it begins to catch up with us. [기출 응용]

04   In this era of globalization, the most important issue facing most countries today is / are the understanding of the differences among cultures. [기출 응용]

05   Rapid growth in the number of college graduates has / have made competition for jobs much more intense than it used to be. [기출 응용]

06   If properly stored, broccoli will stay fresh for up to three days. The best way to store fresh bunches is / are to refrigerate them in an open plastic bag in the vegetable compartment.

[기출 응용]

07   As things change quickly, the importance given to traditional hierarchies and obedience is / are gradually diminished. [기출 응용]

다음 밑줄 친 부분이 어법상 올바르면 ○표, 틀리면 ×표하고 바르게 고치시오.

08   The great scientists are motivated by an inner quest to understand the nature of the universe; the extrinsic reward that matters most to them <u>are</u> the recognition of their peers. [기출 응용]

09   Obviously, some old practices, such as drinking alcohol during a marathon, are no longer recommended, but others, such as a high-carbohydrate meal the night before a competition, <u>has</u> stood the test of time. [기출]

10   The fact that someone is interested enough to help the poor often <u>work</u> wonders. [기출 응용]

11   The observation that old windows are often thicker at the bottom than at the top <u>are</u> often 도전   offered as supporting evidence for the view that glass flows over a time scale of centuries.

[기출 응용]

12   It is a fact that many people using the Internet without the proper protection <u>has</u> been victimized by identity theft and suffered from financial losses.

13   The reason why people start a conversation by talking about the weather or current events <u>are</u> that they are harmless topics and common to everyone.

14 At the beginning of the twenty-first century, the popularity of fine breads and pastries <u>were</u> growing even faster than new chefs could be trained. [기출]

15 Psychologists who study giving behavior <u>have</u> noticed that some people give substantial amounts to one or two charities, while others give small amounts to many charities. [기출]

16 One wise friend of ours who was a parent educator for twenty years <u>advises</u> giving calendars to preschool-age children and writing down all the important events in their life, in part because it helps children understand the passage of time better and how their days will unfold. [기출]

17 Only a fraction of all sound waves are audible. For example, the frequency of sound waves used in ultrasound imaging <u>range</u> above human hearing. [기출]

18 The average life of a street tree surrounded by concrete and asphalt <u>is</u> seven to fifteen years.

[기출 응용]

우리말에 맞도록 괄호 안의 어구를 바르게 배열하시오. (어형 변화 가능, 주어진 어구로만 배열할 것)

19 피부를 타게 하는 태양 광선은 늦은 봄과 초여름에 더 강하다.

(the skin, to burn, the rays, which, intense, from the sun, cause, be, more)

_____ during the late spring and early summer.

20 운동하는 동안의 뇌와 혈류로 전달되는 증가된 산소량은 우리가 피로를 덜 느끼도록 도와준다.

(less fatigued, us, during exercise, help, feel, deliver, to our brain and bloodstream)

The increased amount of oxygen _____

_____ .

<예제> In the back seat of the car next to mine was / were two sweet little boys. [기출]

출제의도 도치구문의 주어 파악하기

해결전략 문장 앞에 나온 부사(구)나 부정어(구)를 주어로 혼동하지 말고 동사와 자리가 바뀐 주어를 찾는다.

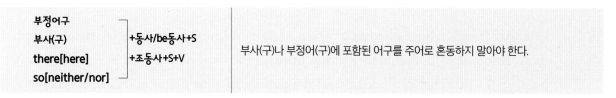

| 부정어구 부사(구) there[here] so[neither/nor] | +동사/be동사+S +조동사+S+V | 부사(구)나 부정어(구)에 포함된 어구를 주어로 혼동하지 말아야 한다. |

- 부정어구: no(-), not, never, little, hardly, scarcely, rarely, not until, not only, only(준부정어), etc.
- 방향, 장소의 부사구 there, here 뒤에는 조동사 do, does, did를 사용하지 않는다.

다음 문장에서 주어를 찾아 밑줄을 긋고 어법상 적절한 표현을 고르시오.

01   Nowhere in this world do / does your salary double in just two weeks.

02   Never has / have he seen such a terrible accident.

03   Only when asked do / does she give her opinion.

04   Under the table was / were several mothballs, and I stepped on one of them.   *mothball: 좀약

05   There has / have been some changes to the schedule.

06   Well, there go / goes my weekend.

07   I haven't read it so I don't know what they say about me and neither do / does I care.

08   As the company grows, so do / does expenses.

Point Exercise

정답 및 해설 p. 51

다음 중 어법상 적절한 표현을 고르시오.

01 Hate is such a strong word. I've never been hated by anyone nor $\boxed{\text{has / have}}$ I hated anybody.

02 Not only $\boxed{\text{do / does}}$ the act of writing a note of appreciation focus your attention on what's right in your life, but the person receiving it will be touched and grateful. [기출 응용]

다음 밑줄 친 부분이 어법상 올바르면 ○표, 틀리면 ✕표하고 바르게 고치시오.

03 Rarely <u>has</u> many schools had the budget to offer quality programs linking classroom instruction to practical application.

04 Due to the recent reconstruction, there <u>is</u> only a handful of tourist attractions open in the area.

05 도전 One company developed what it called a 'technology shelf,' created by a few engineers, on which <u>was</u> placed possible technical solutions that other teams might use in the future. [기출 응용]

06 Only in the last few decades, in the primarily industrially developed countries, <u>have</u> food become so plentiful and easy to obtain as to cause fat-related health problems. [기출 응용]

우리말에 맞도록 괄호 안의 어구를 바르게 배열하시오. (어형 변화 가능, 필요한 어구 추가 가능)

07 상황은 점점 더 나빠지고 있었지만, 그는 자신이 마주한 위험을 거의 깨닫지 못했다.
(he, he, realize, the danger, face)

The situation was getting worse, but little _____ .

도치구문 총정리

CASE 1   부사구+도치

장소·운동의 방향을 나타내는 부사구가 강조를 위해 문두에 오면 주어-동사의 위치가 바뀐다. 도치하지 않은 문장도 틀린 것은 아니다.

Under a tree **was lying one of the biggest men** I had ever seen.

Directly in front of me **stood a great castle**.

CASE 2   부정어+도치

부정어(구)가 강조를 위해 문두에 오면 <조동사+S+V>나 <be동사+S> 형태로 도치된다.

Not a single word **did he say**.

Only with great difficulty **can the giraffe bend** down to graze on the ground.

Under no circumstances **do we give or sell** this personal information to a third party.

At no time **was the president** aware of what was happening.

CASE 3   보어가 문두에 오는 경우

<보어+be동사+S> 형태로 도치된다. 주로 주어가 상대적으로 길 때 문장의 균형상 도치된다.

Wise **is he** who enjoys the show offered by the world.

cf. 목적어: 목적어를 강조하기 위해 문두에 보낸 경우는 주어-동사가 도치되지 않는다.

  What he said **I cannot believe**.

CASE 4   문법적 도치

1. **<so[nor, neither]+V+S>의 도치**

   I had a mustache and **so did he**.

   "I don't like opera." — **"Neither do I."**

2. **<there+V+S>의 도치: 수일치에 유의한다.**

   There **is nothing** impossible for a person of unyielding determination.

   cf. 단, 주어가 대명사인 경우에는 도치되지 않는다.

     There **you are**!

3. **조건절의 도치: if를 생략한 후 주어-동사를 도치시킨다.**

   Were she alive today, she would definitely be an excellent filmmaker.

   (= **If she were** alive today, ~)

   Had it not been for his help, I couldn't have passed the exam.

   (= **If it had** not been for his help, ~)

<조동사+S+V>나 <be동사+S> 형태로 도치된다.

1. not A until B: B하고 나서야 비로소 A하다
Some children **don't** catch on to reading lessons **until** they're seven or eight. [기출 응용]
= *It is* **not until** they're seven or eight that some children catch on to reading lessons.
= **Not until** they're seven or eight *do some children* catch on to reading lessons.

2. not only A but (also) B: A뿐만 아니라 B도
We **not only** lost our money, **but** we were nearly killed.
= **Not only** *did we* lose our money, **but** we were nearly killed.

3. <No sooner+had+S+p.p.+than ...>: ~하자마자 …하다
= <Hardly[Scarcely]+had+S+p.p.+when[before] ...>
I had **no sooner** arrived **than** trouble started.
= **No sooner** *had* I arrived **than** trouble started.
= I had **hardly** arrived **when** trouble started.
= **Hardly** *had* I arrived **when** trouble started.

확인학습

정답 및 해설 p. 52

다음 밑줄 친 부분이 어법상 올바르면 ○표, 틀리면 ✕표하고 바르게 고치시오.

01 No sooner <u>he had been</u> cured of the vice of greed than he fell into the vice of pride.

02 You managed to find out what you're looking for in your life; <u>so I will</u>!

03 At no time <u>he let me down</u>. Every time I saw him working, he was doing his best.

04 The concert was really successful. Seldom <u>I had</u> seen such an impassioned reaction from an audience.

우리말에 맞도록 괄호 안의 어구를 바르게 배열하시오. (어형 변화 가능, 필요한 어구 추가 가능, 중복 사용 가능)

05 그는 집에 도착해서야 레스토랑에 지갑을 두고 왔다는 것을 알았다.
(his wallet, he, find, leave, home, arrive)

Not until _____ in the restaurant.

<예제> Although the first five episodes of the drama had been filmed in black and white, the rest of the show │ was / were │ filmed and broadcast in color.

출제의도 부분 표현이 쓰였을 때의 단수, 복수 구분하기

해결전략 부분/분수 표현이 주어인 경우 뒤따르는 <of+명사(N)>에 수를 일치시키되, <one of+복수명사(N)>는 단수동사로 받는다.

부분/분수 표현 of +명사(N)	다음과 같은 부분이나 분수 표현이 주어인 경우, 뒤따르는 <of + 명사(N)>의 명사(N)에 수를 일치시킨다. some/most/all of + **명사(N)** (~ 중 일부/대부분/전부) the rest/majority of + **명사(N)** (나머지 ~ /대다수의 ~) a portion of + **명사(N)** (약간의 ~) 분수 표현 + **명사(N)**
one of+복수명사(N)	언제나 단수동사로 받는다.

the number of+복수명사+**단수동사** (~의 수)
a number of+복수명사+**복수동사** (다수의 ~)

다음 중 어법상 적절한 표현을 고르시오.

01   When comets pass near the sun, some of the ice │ turn / turns │ to gas.

02   Most of the pages │ has / have │ been written by students themselves.

03   All of the money from the concert │ was / were │ given to charity.

04   The rest of the things │ is / are │ obviously important considerations.

05   The majority of stores │ do / does │ not accept returns on opened software packages.

06   A large portion of his monthly income │ go / goes │ to his children's education.

07   Two-thirds of London citizens │ is / are │ happy with the royal family.

08   One of her pastimes │ is / are │ telling us a lot of stories from legends.

09   The number of foreigners interested in the Korean language │ has / have │ risen dramatically over the past few years. [기출 응용]

10   Accidents can and do happen but there │ is / are │ a number of other reasons for sports injuries. One of the reasons │ is / are │ inadequate or inappropriate preparation.

Point Exercise

정답 및 해설 p. 52

다음 중 어법상 적절한 표현을 고르시오.

01 Some of the ideas about building a sports complex and hosting international games in the city [was / were] quite creative.

02 The instruments were expensive since most of the manufacturing process [was / were] conducted by highly skilled craftspeople. [기출 응용]

03 A medical center reported that a larger portion of their patients (A) [was / were] people who did not have a physical disease but (B) [was / were] seeking psychological help. [기출 응용]

다음 밑줄 친 부분이 어법상 올바르면 ○표, 틀리면 ✕표하고 바르게 고치시오.

04 One of the simplest and most effective ways to build empathy in children <u>are</u> to let them play more on their own. [기출 응용]

05 A number of 'youth friendly' mental health websites <u>have</u> been developed. It would seem, therefore, logical to provide online counselling for young people. [기출]

06 Mental representation is the mental imagery of things that are not actually present to the senses. In general, mental representations can help us learn. Some of the best evidence for this <u>comes</u> from the field of musical performance. [기출]

우리말에 맞도록 괄호 안의 어구를 바르게 배열하시오. (어형 변화 가능, 주어진 어구로만 배열할 것)

07 60명의 사람들이 맛에 있어서 어떤 차이를 식별할 수 있는지를 질문받았다. 결과는 추측들 중에 단 30%만이 정확하다는 것을 보여주었다.

(of the guesses, 30%, correct, be)

Sixty people were asked if they could tell any differences in taste. The result showed that only

_____ .

each와 every는 단수, both는 복수

<예제> In Colonial America, families were usually large, and every boy and girl ⟨was / were⟩ put to work at an early age.

(출제의도) 항상 단수 취급하는 표현과 복수 취급하는 표현 구분하기

(해결전략) each와 every는 단수 취급, both는 복수 취급한다. <the + 형용사>가 '~한 사람들'이란 의미일 때는 복수 취급한다.

단수 취급	• each가 단독으로 문장의 주어일 때 • <each[every] + 단수명사>가 주어일 때
복수 취급	• both가 문장의 주어일 때 • <both + 복수명사> • <the + 형용사 (~한 사람들)> 　e.g. the rich=rich people, the poor=poor people, 　the young=young people, the old[aged, elderly]=old people, the sick=sick people, 　the unemployed=unemployed people (실업자들), the wounded=wounded people (부상자들), 　the blind=blind people (시각장애인들), the deaf=deaf people (청각장애인들), 　the homeless=homeless people (노숙자들), the French=French people (프랑스인들)

다음 중 어법상 적절한 표현을 고르시오.

01　Each of the paragraphs ⟨is / are⟩ joined together by a transition word, phrase or sentence.

02　Each moment with you ⟨is / are⟩ just like a dream to me.

03　Every product we buy ⟨has / have⟩ an effect on the environment. [기출 응용]

04　Both of the firms in the merger ⟨appear / appears⟩ to have very large market shares.

05　Do you think that the rich ⟨are / is⟩ happier than the poor?

• <every+숫자+복수명사>: ~마다
You must take this medicine **every five hours**, or you will be in a very serious situation.
(이 약을 5시간마다 복용해야 합니다. 그렇지 않으면 심각한 상황에 처하게 될 것입니다.)

Point Exercise

정답 및 해설 p. 53

다음 중 어법상 적절한 표현을 고르시오.

01   Entering this garden, you will see dozens of wildflowers of countless varieties covering the ground on | each / both | sides of the path. [기출 응용]

02   The lens of the camera is similar to the human eye; | both / each | are damaged by directly peering at the light. [기출 응용]

03   From mild to wild, every fish (A) | has / have | a distinctive flavor. Chances are there (B) | is / are | a fish in the sea for you. After all, there are plenty of them.

04   In the United States, the emphasis on academic success (A) | is / are | not as strong as in some other countries. This may be because this country has many different cultures, and each culture (B) | define / defines | success in a different way. [기출 응용]

다음 밑줄 친 부분이 어법상 올바르면 ○표, 틀리면 ✕표하고 바르게 고치시오.

05   Each <u>roles of yours make</u> demands on you, and you may be asked to play two or more roles at the same time. [기출 응용]

다음 밑줄 친 부분 중 어법상 <u>틀린</u> 것을 모두 골라 기호를 쓰고 바르게 고치시오.

06   The aged once (A) <u>was</u> the poorest segment of society. However, the growth of Social Security and public and private pensions (B) <u>have</u> improved their income so much in recent decades that the proportion of people 65 and over with incomes below the government's official (C) <u>is</u> now 12.4 percent, compared with the overall national poverty rate of 14.4 percent.

<예제> Throwing unneeded items out only $\boxed{\text{hurts / hurt}}$ for a little while. [기출 응용]

출제의도 주어 자리에 온 명사구나 명사절 파악하기

해결전략 주어 자리에 온 구나 절은 한 덩어리로 보고 단수 취급한다.

단수동사	• 부정사구 / 동명사구 / 접속사[의문사]가 이끄는 명사절이 주어 cf. v-ing(현재분사)+복수명사 주어+**복수동사** • 관계대명사 which나 대명사 주어가 앞 절 전체를 대신할 때 cf. 복수명사 선행사+주격 관계대명사+**복수동사** ~

다음 중 어법상 적절한 표현을 고르시오.

01   To lean out of the window $\boxed{\text{is / are}}$ dangerous.

02   Living plainly and thinking positively $\boxed{\text{is / are}}$ a good thing.

03   Living conditions $\boxed{\text{was / were}}$ terrible; disease was spreading quickly.

04   Whether you leave or not $\boxed{\text{is / are}}$ your choice.

05   Suicides are on the rise, which $\boxed{\text{indicates / indicate}}$ that there's a problem in our society.

06   Indeed, open disagreements and discussions are an excellent way of resolving the differences that inevitably $\boxed{\text{develop / develops}}$ among family members. [기출 응용]

07   Never put your happiness in someone else's hands because that often $\boxed{\text{leads / lead}}$ to disappointment.

08   There are many types of bacteria, such as those found inside your digestive system, which $\boxed{\text{is / are}}$ not harmful.

Point Exercise

정답 및 해설 p. 54

다음 중 어법상 적절한 표현을 고르시오.

01
도전
Who we believe we are is / are a consequence of the choices we make about who we want to be like. [기출 응용]

02 What makes organisms different from the materials that compose them (A) are / is their level of organization. Living things (B) exhibit / exhibits not just one but many layers of biological organization. [기출 응용]

03
도전
Sadly, in many poor areas of the globe, women are not allowed to participate in society, which (A) mean / means half of the knowledge that could improve conditions (B) is / are literally going to waste. [기출 응용]

다음 밑줄 친 부분이 어법상 올바르면 ○표, 틀리면 ✕표하고 바르게 고치시오.

04 Calculating the number of people in large countries <u>are</u> not an easy job, as population can change during a counting period. [기출 응용]

05 In my opinion, the mentally ill deserve voting rights. To exclude those who are already socially isolated from voting <u>destroy</u> our democracy, as it creates a caste system. [기출 응용]

*a caste system: 신분제, 계급 제도

다음 밑줄 친 부분 중에서 어법상 틀린 곳을 찾아 기호를 쓰고 바르게 고치시오.

06 Starting a daycare business (A) <u>allows</u> you to do that while bringing in extra income. It also allows your child to interact with other children, which (B) <u>are</u> good for his social development.

우리말에 맞도록 괄호 안의 어구를 바르게 배열하시오. (어형 변화 가능, 주어진 어구로만 배열할 것)

07 다른 누군가의 기대를 좇아 당신의 인생을 사는 것은 살아가기에 힘든 방법이다.
(a difficult way, expectations, in pursuit of, your life, be, to live, someone else's)

Living _____.

UNIT Exercise

다음 중 어법상 적절한 표현을 고르시오.

01   The rock is so close to the top of the water that all the vessels that try to sail over it boxed(hit / hits) it. [기출]

02   Leonardo da Vinci was one of the most learned and well-rounded persons ever to live. The entire universe from the wing of a dragonfly to the birth of the earth boxed(was / were) the playground of his curious intelligence. [기출]

다음 밑줄 친 부분이 어법상 올바르면 ○표, 틀리면 ✕표하고 바르게 고치시오.

03   Speculations about the meaning and purpose of prehistoric art <u>relies</u> heavily on analogies drawn with modern-day hunter-gatherer societies. [기출 응용]   *speculation: 고찰 **analogy: 유사점

04   It was only in 1837, with the invention of the electric telegraph, that the traditional link between transport and the communication of messages <u>were</u> broken. [기출]

05   Traditional pain-management therapy teaches people to deal with pain by helping them to become more aware of it! However, the key is to help people let go of the constant tension that <u>accompanies</u> their fighting of pain. [기출]

06   If an animal is innately programmed for some type of behavior, then there <u>is</u> likely to be biological clues. [기출 응용]

07   Only if the duty of confidentiality is respected <u>will</u> people feel free to consult lawyers and provide the information required for the lawyer to prepare the client's defense. [기출]

*confidentiality: 비밀 유지

08 Along the New River in West Virginia, the area of vegetation loss on sites used by large commercial rafting companies <u>were</u> more than four times larger than the area on sites used by small groups of fishermen. [기출]

09 Hypnosis might actually be people's beliefs in the power of it that <u>leads</u> them to recall more things: If people believe that they should have better memory under hypnosis, they will try harder to retrieve more memories when hypnotized. [기출 응용]

10 Use a fine mist spray bottle to give humidity after sowing the seeds as it does not disrupt the seeds and <u>water</u> the surface evenly.

11 Not only are humans unique in the sense that they began to use an ever-widening tool set, we are also the only species on this planet that <u>have</u> constructed forms of complexity that use external energy sources. [기출 응용]

12 In the twentieth century, advances in technology, from refrigeration to sophisticated ovens to air transportation that <u>carries</u> fresh ingredients around the world, contributed immeasurably to baking and pastry making. [기출 응용]

13 Some natural resource-rich developing countries tend to create an excessive dependence on their natural resources, which <u>generate</u> a lower productive diversification and a lower rate of growth. [기출 응용]

14
도전
Sudden success or winnings can be very dangerous. Neurologically, chemicals are released in the brain that <u>give</u> a powerful burst of excitement and energy, leading to the desire to repeat this experience. It can be the start of any kind of addiction or manic behavior. [기출 응용]

| Testing Point 27 | '하느냐'와 '되느냐'의 문제 | 전체 기출 빈도 ◆◆◆◆◆ |
| | | 최근 기출 빈도 ◆◆◆◆◇ |

<예제> Excluding guide dogs, companion animals | prohibited / are prohibited | in the museums or the National Zoo.

출제의도 동사의 능동태와 수동태 구분하기

해결전략 주어와 동사의 능동, 수동 관계를 따져 동사의 태를 결정한다. 자동사는 목적어를 취하지 않으므로 수동태로 쓸 수 없다.

능동태 vs. 수동태	타동사가 능동태로 쓰일 때는 뒤에 목적어를 취한다. 타동사 뒤에 목적어가 없다면 일단 수동태 자리가 아닌지 의심한다.
주격 관계대명사절의 동사의 태	주격 관계대명사절의 동사의 태는 선행사와의 능동, 수동 관계를 따져 결정한다.

다음 중 어법상 적절한 표현을 고르시오.

01 X-rays | use / are used | for a variety of purposes.

02 You cannot | divide / be divided | odd numbers evenly by two.

03 Bakers and consumers are looking to reclaim some of the flavors of old-fashioned breads that | lost / were lost | as baking became more industrialized. [기출 응용]

· 1(SV), 2(SVC) 문형을 이루는 자동사는 목적어를 취할 수 없으므로 수동태가 불가능하다.

occur, happen, remain, arrive, seem, rise, result, appear, disappear, consist of, emerge 등

수동태의 복잡한 형태		
진행형 be being p.p.	04	The report is being	print / printed	now.
완료형 have been p.p.	05	Much of our tradition has	forgotten / been forgotten	.
조동사+be p.p.	06	This noise might not	hear / be heard	from a distance.

다음 중 어법상 적절한 표현을 고르시오.

❶ It is a good time to ask questions about salary, benefits, and paid vacation now that you have been offering / offered the position.

❷ The rescue of five children after an earthquake later called / was later called a miracle, considering that hundreds of other children were killed in the same disaster.

❸ The students will conclude the study of the early explorers and settlers of the New World and the discoveries they made / were made .

Guides

❶ 4문형(SVOO)을 수동태로 바꿀 경우, 남은 목적어가 명사 형태로 수동태 뒤에 온다.
give, ask, tell, show, teach, offer, send, pay, lend 등이 해당.
Philip **was given the money** to produce television and radio ads.
(Philip은 텔레비전과 라디오 광고를 제작할 자금을 받았다.)

❷ 명사 보어가 쓰인 5문형(SVOC)을 수동태로 바꿀 경우, 명사 보어가 수동태 뒤에 온다.
consider, think, find, call, name, choose, elect, appoint, make 등이 해당.
Despite some disappointments, the conference **was considered a success**.
(일부 실망스러운 일에도 불구하고, 그 회의는 성공작이라 여겨졌다.)

❸ 타동사 바로 뒤에 목적어가 없지만 능동태인 구문들에 주의한다.
This is the book I **borrowed** ● from the library. (목적격 관계대명사절)
(이것이 내가 도서관에서 빌린 책이다.)
It was her family, not her career, that she **discussed** ● with me yesterday. (목적어 강조 구문)
(그녀가 어제 나와 상의한 것은 그녀의 경력이 아니라 가족이다.)

Point Exercise

정답 및 해설 p. 56

다음 중 어법상 적절한 표현을 고르시오.

01 Successful people have learned the value of simply staying in the game until success
won / is won . [기출 응용]

02 Sometimes your goals remain / are remained unfocused, and therefore unrealized. [기출 응용]

03 도전   A measurement system should be objective. For example, using a tape measure to determine
the distance a javelin threw / was thrown yields very similar results regardless of who reads
the tape. [기출 응용]
    *javelin: 투창

04 For decades, child-rearing advice from psychologists has encouraged / been encouraged the
nighttime separation of baby from parent. [기출 응용]

05 The same technology that astronomers are using / being used to sharpen the images from
telescopes is also giving eye specialists better techniques for studying and correcting human
vision.

06 Some people pretend they are not reacting for the camera. They appear to be interested in
something else. Yet if the camera stays on them long enough, they will slyly check to see if
they are still watching / being watched . [기출 응용]

07 The class will vote by marking their choices on ballots. The votes will count / be counted ,
and the person who gets the most votes becomes the new class president. [기출 응용]

다음 밑줄 친 부분 중 어법상 <u>틀린</u> 것을 찾아 기호를 쓰고 바르게 고치시오.

08 도전   A few people (A) <u>have recognized</u> the value of certain wild plants in Korea. They (B) <u>are
fascinated</u> by the beauty of these plants and (C) <u>have motivated</u> to conserve them after
discovering the threats the plants face. [기출 응용]

우리말에 맞도록 괄호 안의 어구를 바르게 배열하시오. (어형 변화 가능, 필요한 어구 추가 가능)

09 우리는 유통 기한 후에는 음식을 버려야 한다고 어렸을 때부터 배워왔다.
(throw away, since childhood, food, teach, should, that)

We _____ after the expiration date.

빈출 수동태 어구 & 해석에 유의해야 할 자동사

1. 수동의 형태로 흔히 쓰이는 동사

be accustomed to v-ing: v하는 데 익숙하다
be honored to-v: v하는 것이 영광스럽다
be concerned[worried] about: ~에 대해 걱정하다
be dressed in: ~로 차려입다
be located[situated] (in): (~에) 위치해 있다
be obsessed with: ~에 사로잡혀 있다
be seated: 앉다, 앉아 있다
be referred to as: ~로 불리다

We **are honored to** have been chosen as one of the top 100 websites.
(최고의 웹사이트 100개 중 하나로 뽑히게 되어 **영광입니다.**)
People **are concerned about** eating genetically modified foods.
(사람들은 유전자 조작 식품의 섭취**에 대해 걱정한다.**)
Egyptians **were** so **obsessed with** the afterlife that they preserved the dead body as a mummy.
(이집트인들은 사후세계**에** 매우 **집착해서** 시신을 미라로 보존했다.)
Sydney Harbor **is** often **referred to as** the most beautiful harbor in the world.
(시드니 항구는 종종 세계에서 가장 아름다운 항구**로 불린다.**)

2. 능동으로 수동의 의미를 나타내는 동사

This historical adventure novel **sold** half a million copies.
(이 역사 모험 소설은 50만 부가 **팔렸다.**)
The museum does not **open** until 10 a.m. on Sundays.
(그 박물관은 일요일에는 오전 10시가 돼서야 **열린다.**)
The door **closed** right before my eyes.
(문이 바로 내 눈앞에서 **닫혔다.**)
The wind suddenly **changed** from a southerly wind to a northerly wind.
(바람이 갑자기 남풍에서 북풍으로 **바뀌었다.**)

be used to-v vs. be used to v-ing

<예제> The Masai don't slaughter their cattle for food; but if a cow is killed, then the hides are used to ☐ make / making ☐ shoes, clothing, and bed coverings. [기출 응용]

출제의도 be used to-v와 be used to v-ing 구분하기

해결전략 be used to-v와 be used to v-ing를 구분하기 위해 주어, 동사가 수동관계인지 따져본다.

be used to-v	~하는 데 사용되다
be used to + 명사[v-ing]	~하는 데 익숙하다

다음 중 어법상 적절한 표현을 고르시오.

01　Bird songs may be used to ☐ attract / attracting ☐ mates. [기출 응용]

02　We're not used to ☐ spend / spending ☐ a long time in line.

- used to+동사원형: ≪과거의 상태, 습관≫
- would: ≪과거의 습관≫ used to와는 달리, '과거의 상태'를 나타내는 의미로는 쓰이지 않는다.
  We **used to practice** tennis after class. (과거에) ~하곤 했다 (동작) (= would)
  (우리는 방과 후에 테니스를 연습하곤 했다. (지금은 하지 않는다.))
  There **used to be** a statue on the hill. ~했다 (상태) (지금은 아니다)
  (언덕 위에 동상이 하나 있었다. (지금은 없다.))

Point Exercise

정답 및 해설 p. 57

다음 중 어법상 적절한 표현을 고르시오.

01　In Egypt, honey was an ingredient in making mummies. In ancient India, it ☐ used to / was used to ☐ preserve fruit and to make cakes and other foods. [기출 응용]

02　When a big storm came, people who ☐ used to / are used to ☐ quarrel stopped making complaints and fighting. Instead, they pulled together to help one another. [기출 응용]

03　Our bodies are used to ☐ work / working ☐ under the force of gravity. Your heart works hard to get blood and oxygen to move upward, against gravity, to your brain.

다음 중 어법상 적절한 표현을 고르시오.

01 The curriculum of schools these days has grown and changed dramatically, and students leave a lot better prepared for the real world than they used to be / being .

다음 밑줄 친 부분이 어법상 올바르면 ○표, 틀리면 ×표하고 바르게 고치시오.

02 도전 When migration starts, eastern kingbirds are not picky about where they stay, and the different habitats in which they find vary greatly.

03 To show his students how math could really help them, he held a contest to guess how many soda cans the back of a pickup truck held. [기출 응용]

04 Some cities have trained their citizens to separate garbage. People have to put aluminum and plastic containers in different garbage bags. Paper also is keeping separate. [기출 응용]

05 The bacteria are necessary to ripen the cheese. It is its own special flavor and color that it is developed while it is ripening. [기출 응용]

06 Everyone told me that when I turned fifteen some great internal change would (A) be occurred. But nothing (B) happened. [기출 응용]

다음 밑줄 친 부분 중 어법상 틀린 것을 찾아 기호를 쓰고 바르게 고치시오.

07 Wind cannot (A) be seen but its effects can (B) observe by using the senses of sight, sound, and touch, and by tracking bubbles that (C) are carried by the wind.

Testing Point 29   단순과거 vs. 현재완료

전체 기출 빈도   ◆◆◇◇◇
최근 기출 빈도   ◆◇◇◇◇

<예제> In the summer of 2005, he visited / has visited China to participate in a house-building project.

[기출 응용]

출제의도 과거시제와 현재완료시제를 통해 단순시제와 완료시제의 차이 구분하기

해결전략 문장 안에서 시제의 단서가 될 부사구[절]를 찾는다.

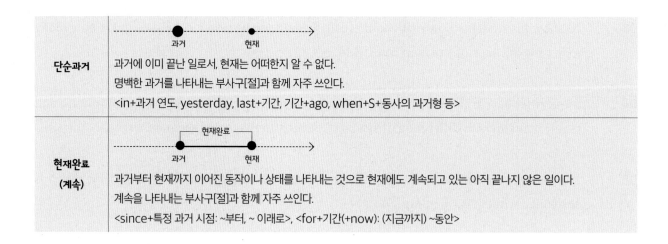

단순과거	과거에 이미 끝난 일로서, 현재는 어떠한지 알 수 없다. 명백한 과거를 나타내는 부사구[절]과 함께 자주 쓰인다. <in+과거 연도, yesterday, last+기간, 기간+ago, when+S+동사의 과거형 등>
현재완료 (계속)	과거부터 현재까지 이어진 동작이나 상태를 나타내는 것으로 현재에도 계속되고 있는 아직 끝나지 않은 일이다. 계속을 나타내는 부사구[절]과 함께 자주 쓰인다. <since+특정 과거 시점: ~부터, ~ 이래로>, <for+기간(+now): (지금까지) ~동안>

다음 중 시제의 단서가 될 부사구[절]에 밑줄을 긋고 어법상 적절한 표현을 고르시오.

01   The market was / has been crowded with shoppers and vendors yesterday morning.

02   The market was / has been crowded with shoppers and vendors since this morning.

03   She retired / has retired from the New Milford Police Department last year.

04   After graduating from university, he joined / has joined the company as a salesperson in 1998.

[기출 응용]

05   Ever since the 1930s, archaeologists believed / have believed that the Tigris and Euphrates valley was the "cradle of civilization."

06   Matt will soon graduate from college. He worked / has worked toward his degree for five years.

Point Exercise

정답 및 해설 p. 58

다음 밑줄 친 부분이 어법상 올바르면 ○표, 틀리면 ╳표하고 바르게 고치시오.

01 Just a few generations ago, most babies born with serious heart problems never <u>have survived</u> to their teens.

02 Since it manufactured its first car in 1955, Korea <u>has grown</u> to be the fifth largest automobile producer in the world. [기출 응용]

03 함정 The eggs <u>were</u> laid when the summer started and, since indoor temperatures are warm, they are hatching.

04 The snow started this morning. It <u>didn't stop</u> snowing yet, so I want to go sledding while it is still light out.

05 To this day, in every country in Latin America, the rate of crime <u>was</u> rising for more than a decade along with the level of crime-related violence.

다음 밑줄 친 부분 중 어법상 틀린 것을 찾아 기호를 쓰고 바르게 고치시오.

06 Women (A) <u>have been</u> first invited to participate in the modern Olympics in 1912. Since then, women's events (B) <u>have become</u> well respected and popular. [기출 응용]

우리말에 맞도록 괄호 안의 어구를 바르게 배열하시오. (어형 변화 가능, 필요한 어구 추가 가능)

07 꿀은 좋은 맛과 치유 속성 때문에 선사 시대 이래로 인간에 의해 채집되고 섭취되어 왔다.
(by humans, consume, since prehistoric times, collect)

Honey _____
because of its delicious taste and its healing properties.

　현재완료 vs. 과거완료

<예제> The police realized that they │ have made / had made │ a terrible mistake. The men were Italian onion-sellers and their bags were full of onions! [기출 응용]

출제의도 현재완료와 과거완료시제 구분하기

해결전략 현재완료(계속: 과거에서 현재)와 과거완료(계속: 대과거에서 과거)는 동작이나 상태가 시작되고 계속된 기간의 시점 차이이며, 과거완료(대과거)는 시간상으로 먼저 일어난 일임을 나타내기도 한다.

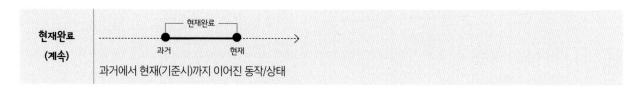

01　They **have been** friends since they *were* kids.

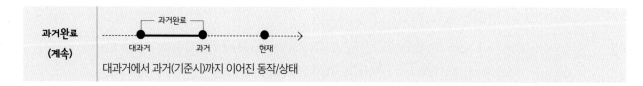

02　She **had been** ill *for a week* when I last *met* her.

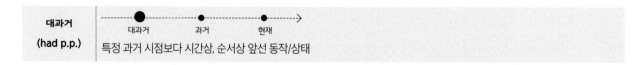

03　The only way to learn about early immigrants *was* to read what **had been written**.

- 보통, 일어난 순서대로 나열할 때는 먼저 일어난 일을 굳이 대과거로 표현하지 않는다.
  I **cooked** lunch and made a cake. (나는 점심을 요리했고 케이크를 만들었다.)

- 접속사로 인해 순서가 분명한 경우에도 굳이 대과거로 표현하지 않는 경우가 많다.
  Did she **leave** a message *before* she went to the restaurant? (메시지 남긴 것이 더 이전의 일)
  (그녀가 식당으로 떠나기 전에 메시지를 남겼니?)

- 현재[과거]완료시제는 '동작/상태의 계속'뿐 아니라 '완료, 결과, 경험' 등의 의미도 나타낸다.

Point Exercise

정답 및 해설 p. 59

다음 중 어법상 적절한 표현을 고르시오.

01 My mother came home and asked me what I | have / had | been doing. Laughing, I answered, "Oh, just hanging around." [기출 응용]

02 The crew members | have / had | been trapped beneath the ship for a number of hours when their oxygen ran out.

다음 밑줄 친 부분 중 어법상 **틀린** 것을 찾아 기호를 쓰고 바르게 고치시오.

03 Frodo woke and found himself lying in bed. The ceiling looked different from what he (A) had seen before. At first he thought that he (B) has slept late. But soon after, he realized it was not his home. [기출 응용]

우리말에 맞도록 괄호 안의 어구를 바르게 배열하시오. (어형 변화 가능, 필요한 어구 추가 가능, 중복 사용 불가)

04 집에 도착하자마자, 나는 마실 것을 사는 것을 잊어버린 것을 깨달았다.
(drink, buy, realize, forget, something, I)

As soon as I got home, I _____.

| **Further Study** |

미래완료

미래완료는 과거 및 현재에서 미래(기준시)까지 이어진 동작/상태를 나타낸다.

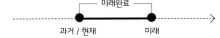

They **will have been married** for thirty years next month.
(그들은 다음 달이면 결혼한 지 30년이 될 것이다.)

나타내는 때(Time)와 시제(Tense)가 반드시 일치하지는 않는다

전체 기출 빈도 ◆◇◇◇◇
최근 기출 빈도 ◆◇◇◇◇

<예제> Cooking broccoli is extremely easy: all you have to do is boil it in water just until it is / will be tender, three to five minutes. [기출 응용]

출제의도 현재시제가 미래시제를 대신하는 경우 구분하기

해결전략 시간, 조건을 나타내는 부사절에서는 현재시제로 미래를 대신한다.

현재시제 = 미래의 때	시간이나 조건을 나타내는 부사절에서는 현재시제로 미래를 나타낸다. • 시간, 조건 접속사: when, while, until, till, once, as soon as, after, before, by the time, if, unless, once(일단 ~하면), as long as(~하는 한), in case(~할 경우를 대비해서) 등
미래시제 = 미래의 때	명사절에서는 원칙적으로 미래시제로 미래를 나타낸다. • 명사절: 문장에서 주어, 목적어, 보어가 된다. '~인지 (아닌지)'를 의미하는 if[whether]나 when(언제) 같은 의문사도 명사절을 이끌 수 있다.

다음 빈칸에 be동사의 알맞은 형태를 쓰시오.

01   Registrations will be canceled if tuition fees due _____ not paid.

02   Could you please tell me if the Beijing flight _____ arriving on time?

03   Your future refrigerator will send you a message when you _____ running low on milk.

04   To be well prepared, team members need to know when the meeting _____ held.

Point Exercise

정답 및 해설 p. 60

다음 밑줄 친 부분이 어법상 올바르면 ○표, 틀리면 ✕표하고 바르게 고치시오.

01 If you <u>will drive</u> yourself to a new place by following directions, you'll probably remember how to get there days or even weeks later. [기출 응용]

02 You feel lonely. You miss friends and socializing. You wonder if you <u>ever become</u> socially active again. Sure you can, but whether you actually will is up to you.

03 When you <u>will take</u> the test, you will mark your answers on a separate machine-readable answer sheet.

04 Once forests <u>are</u> gone, polluted waters will flow directly into streams and create deadly conditions for stream organisms.

우리말에 맞도록 괄호 안의 어구를 바르게 배열하시오. (어형 변화 가능, 주어진 어구로만 배열할 것, 중복 사용 가능)

05 트라우마를 겪지 않으면 네가 얼마나 강한지 진정으로 알지 못할 것이다.
(you, trauma, know, mighty, go through, how, genuinely, are, won't)

Unless you _____ .

| Further Study |

Time(때)과 Tense(시제)가 일치하지 않는 또 다른 경우

1. 현재의 습관·사실, 일반적 진리: 주절이 과거라도 종속절(주로 명사절)에 현재시제

He **told** me that he **takes** a multivitamin pill every morning.
(그는 매일 아침 종합 비타민제를 먹고 있다고 내게 말했다. (현재의 습관))

People **were** aware that the virus **is** not transmitted by sharing eating or drinking utensils.
(사람들은 그 바이러스가 식음료기를 같이 쓴다고 전염되지는 않는다는 것을 알고 있었다. (일반적 진리))

2. 가까운 시일에 확정된 일정/계획: 현재형이나 현재진행형 = 미래

A new music school **opens** in the village *this month*.
(새 음악 학교가 이번 달 그 마을에서 개교한다.)

All-Star Sporting Equipment **is having** a sale on all equipment in the store *next month*.
(올스타 스포츠용사는 다음 달에 매장의 모든 용품을 대상으로 할인 판매를 할 것이다.)

가정법 문제의 핵심은
실제 나타내는 때와의 시제 불일치

<예제> The situation | might be / might have been | quite different if they had known that the young musician was a world-famous pianist. [기출 응용]

출제의도 가정법 과거와 과거완료 구분하기

해결전략 현재나 과거 중 어느 때를 가정하는지 문맥을 살피고 조건절과 주절의 시제의 짝이 맞는지도 확인한다.

가정법 과거	If+S+동사과거형, S+조동사과거형+동사원형 would, could, might	현재 사실의 반대, 또는 현재나 미래에 일어날 것 같지 않은 일
가정법 과거 완료	If+S+had p.p., S+조동사과거형+have p.p. would, could, might	과거 사실의 반대, 또는 과거에 일어났을 것 같지 않은 일

01 If he **were** smarter, he **could** probably **figure out** what's wrong.

02 If Wills **had allowed** himself to become frustrated by his mistakes, he **would have** never **set** any records. [기출 응용]

• 가정법 문장을 종속절로 가져올 때 주절의 시제에 따라 가정법 시제를 변화시키지 않는다.
He said, "I **would** go if I **were** not ill." ("아프지만 않으면 갈 텐데."라고 그가 말했다.)
He said that he **would** go if he **were** not ill. (아프지만 않으면 갈 것이라고 그가 말했다.)

Point Exercise

정답 및 해설 p. 60

다음 중 어법상 적절한 표현을 고르시오.

01 If this election had been held several months ago, I would not | hesitate / have hesitated | to vote for that candidate. But things have changed now.

02 A police officer who was on the beach said that if Clara | hasn't / hadn't | reacted so quickly and decisively, there would have been two drownings instead of one. [기출 응용]

03
도전 He learned that their religion was the center of their lives. He believed that if Europeans tried to change the religions of Africans or any of their customs, the Africans' lives | would be / would have been | worse than before. [기출 응용]

<I wish+가정법> & <as if[though]+가정법>

1. <I wish+가정법> (Subjunctive after wish)

소망하는 시점과 소망 내용의 시점이 일치하면 가정법 과거를, 소망하는 시점보다 소망 내용의 시점이 더 먼저이면
가정법 과거완료를 쓴다.

I *wish* you **were** here with us. (**현재** 시점에 **현재**의 일을 소망)

(네가 여기에 우리와 함께 있으면 좋으련만.)

I *wished* you **were** there with us. (**과거** 시점에 **과거**의 일을 소망)

(네가 거기에 우리와 함께 있었으면 좋았으련만.)

I *wish* I **had** not **met** you. (**현재** 시점에 **과거**의 일을 소망)

(내가 너를 만나지 않았으면 좋으련만.)

I *wished* I **had** not **met** you. (**과거** 시점에 **더 과거**의 일을 소망)

(내가 너를 만나지 않았으면 좋았으련만.)

2. <as if[though]+가정법> (Subjunctive after as if / as though)

의미상 as if 앞뒤 동작의 시점이 일치하면 가정법 과거를, as if 뒤에 오는 동작의 시점이 먼저이면 가정법 과거완료를 쓴다.

You *sound* as if you **were** my mother.

(너는 마치 우리 엄마인 것처럼 말하는구나.)

You *sounded* as if you **were** my mother.

(너는 마치 우리 엄마인 것처럼 말했어.)

You *look* as if you **had seen** a ghost!

(너 마치 귀신을 본 것 같은 표정이구나!)

You *looked* as if you **had seen** a ghost!

(너 마치 귀신을 본 것 같은 표정이었어!)

cf. as if[though]가 이끄는 절에는 직설법이 올 수도 있다.

It looks *as if* it's **going to snow**.

(눈이 올 것처럼 보인다.)

All members of the school community feel *as though* they **belong** and **can make** a positive
contribution to the school. [기출 응용]

(학교의 모든 구성원은 마치 자신들이 학교에 소속돼 있고 긍정적인 공헌을 할 수 있는 것처럼 느낀다.)

다음 중 어법상 적절한 표현을 고르시오.

01 Through poetry we can feel the loves and losses, joys and sorrows, and hopes and fears of others
almost as if they ⏐ were / had been ⏐ our own. [기출 응용]

02 I wish that in my youth I ⏐ had / had had ⏐ a teacher of good sense to direct my reading.

03 He simply ignored the first resolution as though he ⏐ never made / had never made ⏐ it.

당위성을 내포한 that절에는 (should+)동사원형 | 전체 기출 빈도 ◆◇◇◇◇
최근 기출 빈도 ◆◆◇◇◇

<예제> I insisted that everyone | be / was | fully ready for the meetings so that they could go well.

출제의도 요구, 주장, 제안, 명령의 의미일 때 가정법 사용 알기

해결전략 주절이 <요구, 주장, 제안, 명령>의 의미일 경우, that절에 당위성이 내포되면 <(should+)동사원형> 형태의 가정법 시제를 써야 한다.

(should+) 동사원형	that절에 '~해야만 한다'라는 당위성이 내포되면 <(should+)동사원형>을 쓴다. ・당위성이 내포되는 that절을 이끄는 <요구·주장·제안·명령>의 동사 insist / recommend / demand / request / order(~을 명령하다) / suggest / advise / ask(~을 요구하다) / propose / command / urge 단, that절에 '~해야만 한다'라는 당위성이 내포되지 않으면 직설법 시제를 쓴다.

that절의 '당위성' 여부를 판단하여 어법상 적절한 표현을 고르시오.

01   The president insisted that the operation | was / should be | kept secret. [기출 응용]

02   Many witnesses insisted that the accident | take / took | place on the crosswalk. [기출 응용]

03   I suggested that the matter | was / be | discussed in the meeting.

04   Research suggests that women | are / be | generally more inclined to feel empathy.

Point Exercise

정답 및 해설 p. 61

다음 중 어법상 적절한 표현을 고르시오.

01 Dentists recommend that toothbrushes are / be replaced approximately every 3–4 months or sooner because the bristles become frayed with use.

02 In order to prevent such diseases as cancer and diabetes, it is advised that everyone over the age of 25 has / have a regular physical examination. [기출 응용]

03 The study suggests that we find / should find our own faces charming because they remind us of the faces we looked at constantly when we were babies — Mom's face and Dad's. [기출 응용]

다음 밑줄 친 부분이 어법상 올바르면 ○표, 틀리면 ✕표하고 바르게 고치시오.

04 The evidence suggests that early human populations <u>preferred</u> the fat and organ meat of the animal over its muscle meat. [기출]

다음 밑줄 친 부분 중 어법상 틀린 곳을 찾아 기호를 쓰고 바르게 고치시오.

05
도전 When I suggest he (A) <u>studies</u> for the civil service exam, he insists that he (B) <u>doesn't have</u> time and that he is too busy with hobbies. [기출 응용]

우리말에 맞도록 괄호 안의 어구를 바르게 배열하시오. (어형 변화 가능, 주어진 어구로만 배열할 것)

06 어떤 언어학자들은 언어 학습이 초등학교에서 가능한 한 빨리 시작해야 한다고 권고한다.
(language learning, as ... as possible, that, begin, urge, early)

Some linguists _____

in elementary schools.

조동사는 시제와 의미를 파악하라

전체 기출 빈도 ◆◆◇◇◇
최근 기출 빈도 ◆◇◇◇◇

<예제> I regret having paid little attention to him. In other words, I should pay / should have paid more attention to him. [기출 응용]

출제의도 조동사의 시제와 의미 차이 구분하기

해결전략 문맥으로 조동사가 실제로 나타내는 시제와 의미를 확인한다.

<조동사+동사원형>	현재의 가능성, 추측
<조동사+have p.p.>	과거의 가능성, 추측

• might, could, should, would는 형태가 과거형이지만 가능성, 추측을 의미할 때는 현재나 미래에 대한 것이다.

01   I have a dog, and I'm wondering if that **would be** a problem.

02   A few years ago, that **would have been** a problem.

must have p.p.	~했음이 틀림없다
may[might] have p.p.	~했을지도 모른다
cannot have p.p.	~했을 리가 없다
should have p.p.	~했어야 했는데 (하지 않았다) [후회, 유감]

다음 중 어법상 적절한 표현을 고르시오.

03   He must / cannot have been very tired since he had worked for so long.

04   Thousands of New Yorkers cannot / may have been late to work Tuesday because emergency brakes were pulled on their trains.

05   His chest may / cannot have been injured; otherwise, he would not have such strength to cry out.

06   There are so many places that I must / should have visited when I was a student in Beijing in the mid-1980s.

• 조동사가 나타내는 가능성, 추측의 정도: might < may < could < can < should < would < will < must

Point Exercise

정답 및 해설 p. 62

다음 중 어법상 적절한 표현을 고르시오.

01 While jury selection is proceeding, everyone who has been summoned to appear at jury duty
must arrive / must have arrived by nine o'clock in the morning and assemble in the jury
room. [기출 응용]

02 The Great Chicago Fire began in a barn that housed a cow belonging to a woman named
Mrs. O'Leary. It was thought that Mrs. O'Leary's cow must knock / must have knocked over
a gas lamp. [기출 응용]

03 A new study defies the conventional wisdom that stars spend their entire lifespans in the
same galactic region. According to it, our sun, which lies 26,000 light years from the center
of the Milky Way, cannot / may have been born in a different part of the galaxy and later
migrated to its current position.

다음 밑줄 친 부분 중 어법상 틀린 것을 찾아 기호를 쓰고 바르게 고치시오.

04 We often hear stories of ordinary people who, if education had focused on creativity,
(A) <u>could have become</u> great artists or scientists. Those victims of education (B) <u>should
receive</u> more encouragement when they were at school. [기출 응용]

<조동사+have p.p.>를 사용하여 우리말에 맞도록 괄호 안의 어구를 바르게 배열하시오. (어형 변화 가능, 필요한 어구 추가 가능)

05 멜리사는 그 시험을 위해 공부하지 않아서 그것에 A를 받으리라고 예상했을 리가 없다.
(expect, get an A, on it)

Mellissa didn't study for the test, so she _____ .

조동사가 포함된 빈출 표현

CASE 1 | CAN

1. cannot help + v-ing
    cannot (choose) but + 동사원형   ~하지 않을 수 없다
    have no choice[option, alternative] but + to-v

    Just listen to his songs, and you **cannot help *being moved*** by his romantic voice.
    When he said, "I love you," I **could not but *respond*** with a smile to his words.
    The deer **had no choice but *to replace*** their regular food with anything given by the people nearby.

[기출 응용]

2. cannot ~ too: 아무리 ~해도 지나치지 않다, ~해야 마땅하다
    The importance of experiments in science classes **cannot** be emphasized **too** much.
    = ~ in science classes **cannot** be **over**emphasized. [기출 응용]
    cf. I **can never** thank you **enough**.
    ref. We **cannot** think of the classical Greeks **without** thinking of Plato.

3. cannot A and B: A와 B를 동시에 할 수는 없다
    You **cannot** have your cake **and** eat it, too.

CASE 2 | MAY

1. may well: ⅰ. 아마 ~일 것이다 (추측을 강조)
              ⅱ. 충분히 ~할 수도 있다, ~하는 것이 당연하다 (허락을 강조)
    The company **may well *go*** bankrupt by the end of the year.
    Your hard work **may well *pay off*** in the near future.

2. may[might] as well: ~하는 편이 낫다, ~하는 것이 좋다
    You **may as well *go*** to work early.
    You **might as well *keep*** it there. I'll pick up another umbrella today.
    I looked around and thought that I **might as well *have*** something to eat.
    cf. I thought I **had better *have*** something to eat before it got dark.

다음 중 어법상 적절한 표현을 고르시오.

01 He was seriously injured in the fire and it remains unclear if he is / will be able to return to work at the company next month.

02 Since your dog was used to getting attention when he whined in the past, he will intensify the whining once he notices / will notice you start ignoring it.

03 The supervisor has / had worked with us for seven years when he suddenly announced his resignation.

04 At present, there are over 475 people who have gone into outer space. This number will climb much faster after commercial flights to outer space begin / will begin .

다음 밑줄 친 부분이 어법상 올바르면 ○표, 틀리면 ×표하고 바르게 고치시오.

05 Unfortunately, there's no way to know whether the memories hypnotized people retrieve are true or not — unless of course we know exactly what the person should be able to remember. But if we <u>knew</u> that, then we'd have no need to use hypnosis in the first place! [기출]

06 If a food contains more sugar than any other ingredient, government regulations require that sugar <u>be</u> listed first on the food label. [기출응용]

다음 밑줄 친 부분 중 어법상 <u>틀린</u> 것을 모두 찾아 기호를 쓰고 바르게 고치시오.

07 Thirty years ago, the town (A) <u>has had</u> one of the highest crime rates in the county. Since then, the crime rate (B) <u>dropped</u> dramatically, and Flatsburg now has one of the lowest crime rates in the county. Economists argue that this dramatic decline is the result of new factories that (C) <u>opened</u> about thirty years ago in Flatsburg.

❶ 일치 ▶ UNIT 08

• 동사 바로 1 _____ 에 나온 주어의 수식어구, 삽입어구를 주어로 혼동하지 말아야 한다.

• 문장 앞에 나온 부사(구)나 부정어구(구)를 주어로 혼동하지 말고 동사와 자리가 바뀐 주어를 찾는다.

• 부분/분수 표현이 주어인 경우, 뒤따르는 <명사(N)>에 동사의 수를 일치시키되, <one of + 복수명사(N)>는 언제나
  2 _____ 동사로 받는다.

• the number of + 복수명사 + 3 _____ 동사 (~의 수)
  a number of + 복수명사 + 4 _____ 동사 (다수의 ~)

• each와 every는 5 _____ 취급, both는 복수 취급한다. <the + 형용사>가 '~한 사람들'이란 의미일 때는
  6 _____ 취급한다.

• 주어 자리에 온 구나 절은 한 덩어리로 보고 7 _____ 취급한다. 관계대명사 which나 대명사 주어가 앞 절 전체를 대신할
  때도 8 _____ 취급한다.

❷ 태 ▶ UNIT 09

• 주어와 동사의 능동, 수동 관계를 따져 동사의 태를 결정한다. 9 _____ 는 목적어를 취하지 않으므로 수동태로 쓸 수
  없다. 주격 관계대명사절의 동사는 10 _____ 와의 능동, 수동 관계를 따져 결정한다.

• be used to-v와 be used to v-ing를 구분하기 위해 주어, 동사가 11 _____ 관계인지 따져본다.

❸ 시제, 법과 조동사 ▶ UNIT 10

• 문장 안에서 단순과거 또는 현재완료(계속) 시제의 단서가 될 12 _____ 를 찾는다.

• 대과거는 시간상으로 13 _____ 임을 나타낸다.

• 시간, 조건을 나타내는 부사절에서는 14 _____ 로 미래를 대신한다.

• 가정법 문제는 현재나 과거 중 어느 때를 가정하는지 문맥을 살피고 조건절과 주절의 시제의 짝이 맞는지도 확인한다.

• 주절이 <요구, 주장, 제안, 명령>의 의미일 경우, that절에 당위성이 내포되면 15 _____ 형태의 가정법
  시제를 써야 한다. 단, that절에 '~해야만 한다'라는 당위성이 내포되지 않으면 직설법 시제를 쓴다.

• 문맥으로 조동사가 실제로 나타내는 시제와 의미를 확인한다.

다음 밑줄 친 부분이 어법상 올바르면 ○표, 틀리면 ✕표하고 바르게 고치시오.

01   If a colleague doesn't understand your idea, you are <u>being given</u> an important message. Maybe your view of a problem that you think you are solving is not shared by other coworkers.

02   If farmers in developing countries were given decent prices for their produce, they would <u>have been</u> able to enjoy better living conditions.

03   The local government recommends that all dog owners <u>are</u> required to post a sign indicating that a dog lives on the premises.

04   Some people's temperatures rise very slowly at first and reach a peak in the late afternoon or evening. Not until quite late in the day <u>does</u> their temperatures begin to drop. [기출 응용]

05   Some bees are referred to as cuckoo bees, because they are similar to cuckoo birds, which lay an egg in the nest of another bird and <u>leaves</u> it for that bird to raise. [기출 응용]

다음 밑줄 친 부분 중 어법상 틀린 것을 찾아 기호를 쓰고 바르게 고치시오.

06
도전
City residents who live right beneath flight paths (A) <u>suffer from</u> the loud noise of low-flying aircraft. This situation would be considerably improved if airports (B) <u>are</u> built somewhere in the countryside, where fewer people would (C) <u>be affected</u>. [기출 응용]

PART
V

실전 모의고사

1   (A), (B), (C)의 각 네모 안에서 어법에 맞는 표현으로 가장 적절한 것은?

Among the explanations for our nation's high divorce rate (A) is / are that we have such strong expectations of marriage. We expect our spouse to be a lover, a friend, a counselor, a career person, and a parent. For example, in one survey (B) conducted / conducting by Epstein in 1981, unhappily married people, especially men, expressed unrealistic expectations about marriage. On the other hand, those with happy marriages showed the most respect toward their spouses. In short, the most important thing that happily married couples have in common is not to expect too much but (C) respected / to respect each other.

	(A)		(B)		(C)
①	is	—	conducted	—	respected
②	is	—	conducted	—	to respect
③	is	—	conducting	—	to respect
④	are	—	conducting	—	respected
⑤	are	—	conducting	—	to respect

2   다음 글의 밑줄 친 부분 중, 어법상 틀린 것은?

What does the phrase "healthy eating" mean to you? A decade ago, that phrase meant something completely different to me than it ① does now. I ② used to believe healthy eating meant consuming only a small amount of fat or calories for each meal. I had no idea how to read the list of ingredients on a food item, nor ③ did I understand the importance of looking at the Nutrition Facts label. I only concentrated on ④ what I shouldn't eat. However, my extreme dieting eventually had a detrimental impact on my health. I realized that focusing on nutritious whole foods that I should eat ⑤ to allow me to have a healthy, balanced diet without feeling deprived. In the words of Hippocrates, "Let food be your medicine and medicine be your food."

3 다음 밑줄 친 부분 중 어법상 **틀린** 것을 두 개 찾아 기호를 쓰고 바르게 고치시오.

Nicknames and their associated identities, in the emerging medium of online communication, ⓐ <u>has</u> become an important means of identifying the participants in chat rooms and newsgroups. H. Bays, a sociolinguist, observes that online, a nickname is anything from numbers and punctuation to a highly personal or expressive name and ⓑ <u>containing</u> numerous clues to gender, age, music and sports interests. Look at *snowwhite12*, *lion66*, *musiclover33*, and *Birdie_sunneyman*, for example. She further points out that the nickname is the first sign of individuality ⓒ <u>when</u> one encounters another participant. It serves as a first impression and shows the "face" ⓓ <u>that</u> its creator wants everyone else to "see" online. [기출 응용]

4 다음 밑줄 친 부분 중 어법상 **틀린** 것을 모두 찾아 기호를 쓰고 바르게 고치시오.

I remember one of the smartest I.T. executives for whom I ever worked strongly ⓐ <u>resisting</u> the movement to measure programmer productivity that was popular at the time. He said that you can never tell whether they are working by looking at them. Picture two programmers ⓑ <u>work</u> side by side. One is leaning back in his chair with his eyes ⓒ <u>closing</u> and his feet on the desk. The other is working hard, ⓓ <u>typing</u> code into his computer. The one with his feet up could be thinking, and the other one may be too busy ⓔ <u>typing</u> to give it enough thought. In the end, the busy typist could well produce ten times as many lines of code as the thinker, which contain twice as many new problems as the thinker's. But they would reward him and punish his thoughtful neighbor. [기출 응용]

실전 모의고사 | 2회

1 (A), (B), (C)의 각 네모 안에서 어법에 맞는 표현으로 가장 적절한 것은?

The majority of the plants we have in our house or office (A) $\boxed{\text{is / are}}$ actually from the tropics. They thrive in humidity, and most houses and offices aren't very humid. Misting isn't a true solution, (B) $\boxed{\text{although / despite}}$ what you may have heard. It's embarrassing for both you and the plant, and the water evaporates immediately anyway. A cool way to solve the humidity problem is to fill a little shallow dish with water and pebbles and (C) $\boxed{\text{places / place}}$ it near your plant or under it. The water evaporates slowly off the rocks — much less quickly than it will off the plant's leaves — and provides a little more moisture in the air around your plant.

	(A)		(B)		(C)
①	is	—	despite	—	places
②	is	—	although	—	places
③	is	—	despite	—	place
④	are	—	although	—	place
⑤	are	—	despite	—	place

2 다음 글의 밑줄 친 부분 중, 어법상 틀린 것은?

A cat typically lands on his feet when he falls from a high place. His body reflexively corrects its course ① <u>so that</u> by the time he reaches the ground, his feet are positioned to hit first. A cat who is falling from great heights ② <u>begins</u> to shift his balance immediately after his fall begins. His body figures out which side should be up, and he begins ③ <u>rotating</u> his head until he's facing that way. Next his spine follows as he arches his back; then he positions his front feet and back legs under him, with his front paws placed near his face to protect ④ <u>it</u> from the ground's impact. Cats are also born with flexible backbones. While humans have just 24 vertebrae, they have 30, which ⑤ <u>contribute</u> to their flexibility. However, their tails play no role during a fall. A cat without a tail can still successfully land on its feet. *vertebrae: 척추뼈

3 다음 밑줄 친 부분 중 어법상 틀린 것을 두 개 찾아 기호를 쓰고 바르게 고치시오.

A centenarian is a person who is at least 100 years old. Centenarians are honored by television shows like NBC's Today, ⓐ <u>where</u> a person aged at least 100 is shown on the weather report each day. When this practice first started many years ago, there were few centenarians and everyone wanted ⓑ <u>to honor</u> like them. Recently, however, the number of centenarians has increased so dramatically ⓒ <u>which</u> those shown are randomly selected. The last census reported that there were over 35,000 centenarians ⓓ <u>living</u> in the United States, more than double the number ten years ago. The U.S. Census Bureau estimates that within a hundred years, there will be more than one million centenarians in the country.

*centenarian: 백세인(100세(이상)인 사람)

4 다음 밑줄 친 부분 중 어법상 틀린 것을 모두 찾아 기호를 쓰고 바르게 고치시오.

There is a fascinating history to the word "gossip," which tells us ⓐ <u>how</u> isolated we have become in our communities. In medieval Ireland, ⓑ <u>because</u> the men spent the days in the fields and so many women died in childbirth or of disease, there were few adults to watch over the children. It became the custom for anyone in the community who saw or spoke to a child in the course of the day's work to pass on ⓒ <u>that</u> information immediately to anyone else in the community. That constant concern with the children ⓓ <u>called</u> "gossiping" the children, and it was meant to keep them under the concerned watch of the adult community. Now when we ask our children where they are going and the answer comes back "To the mall" or just "Out," ⓔ <u>that</u> is often where parental control stops. And, of course, "gossip" has become a negative word, ⓕ <u>implied</u> inappropriate interest in another's affairs.

1 (A), (B), (C)의 각 네모 안에서 어법에 맞는 표현으로 가장 적절한 것은?

Tossing stuff out is difficult for many people. Professional organizers are prepared for this resistance and wield an array of techniques to break (A) it / them down. One trick is pushing the client into throwing as many items as possible into large, black trash bags or big cardboard boxes that quickly mask the items and can be whisked away before second thoughts set in. Another is having the client (B) kept / keep a photograph of the object as a substitute for the item. One organizer says that when a client exhibits a strong emotional attachment to an item that's a candidate for the trash, she makes the client talk to the item as if it were a friend (C) embarrass / to embarrass the client into realizing how silly it is to be overly tied to an object. All organizers reassure clients that they'll ultimately be much happier having gotten rid of their things.

	(A)		(B)		(C)
①	it	—	keep	—	embarrass
②	it	—	keep	—	to embarrass
③	it	—	kept	—	to embarrass
④	them	—	kept	—	to embarrass
⑤	them	—	keep	—	embarrass

2 다음 글의 밑줄 친 부분 중, 어법상 틀린 것은?

Human beings differ in many ways and have a variety of tastes; different things appeal more to one person than to ① another. You may never feel about Newton the way you feel about Shakespeare, either because you may be able to read Newton so well that you do not have to read him again, or because mathematical systems of the world just do not have all that ② much appeal to you. Or, if they ③ are — Charles Darwin is an example of such a person — then Newton may be one of the handful of books that ④ are great for you, and not Shakespeare. There is no particular book or group of books that must be great for you, but you should seek out the ⑤ few books that have value for you.

3 다음 밑줄 친 부분 중 어법상 **틀린** 것을 두 개 찾아 기호를 쓰고 바르게 고치시오.

One of the most significant advances during the Renaissance ⓐ <u>were</u> the development of a new attitude toward the acquisition of knowledge itself. The scientific method worked to understand the world through empirical observation and experiment and to provide rational explanations. Considerable progress ⓑ <u>was made</u> in such fields as astronomy, physics, and anatomy, but science soon came into conflict with the Roman Catholic Church. When Copernicus, on the basis of his observations, suggested that the Sun, and not the Earth, ⓒ <u>be</u> the point about which the planets revolved, the Church banned his book. Galileo demonstrated that the planets are held in their orbits by physical laws and not by angels, which led to ⓓ <u>him</u> spending the last eight years of his life under house arrest. Such ideas were eventually accepted by the scientific community, nevertheless, largely through the power of the ⓔ <u>recently</u> invented printing press.

4 다음 밑줄 친 부분 중 어법상 **틀린** 것을 모두 찾아 기호를 쓰고 바르게 고치시오.

The neurotransmitter dopamine moves between neurons and synapses in different areas of the brain that ⓐ <u>control</u> the way in which people sleep, eat, and move, among other actions. When people experience external stimuli, dopamine is released into neural pathways to the reward system. This tells people ⓑ <u>that</u> they're doing is pleasing, and they should continue to do it. For example, research shows that screens cause dopamine to be released into the pathways, which wears down these pathways in the brain and ⓒ <u>increase</u> the desire for greater stimuli. The rush of dopamine experienced by children watching screens ⓓ <u>strains</u> their brain's reward system before it has fully developed. Their brains crave more and more dopamine while producing less dopamine naturally, which possibly makes it more difficult for them to feel joy from natural causes. *neurotransmitter: 신경 전달 물질 **synapse: 신경 접합부, 시냅스

실전 모의고사 │ 4회

1 (A), (B), (C)의 각 네모 안에서 어법에 맞는 표현으로 가장 적절한 것은?

Nature seems to be constantly changing. If we observe nature closely, however, we discover (A) [what / that] there is constant tension between change and balance. In the case of human beings, the general shape and size of our body remains relatively constant while the cells within it are continually (B) [replacing / being replaced]. Likewise, the forest remains a forest, even while individual trees and grasses are removed by death and replaced by birth. The dead bodies of organisms in the forest are broken down and turned into soil, which in turn (C) [nourishes / nourish] other organisms. The elements of nature are continually changing, but nature itself remains constant. [기출 응용]

(A)	(B)	(C)
① what —	replacing —	nourish
② what —	being replaced —	nourishes
③ that —	replacing —	nourishes
④ that —	being replaced —	nourishes
⑤ that —	being replaced —	nourish

2
도전

다음 글의 밑줄 친 부분 중, 어법상 틀린 것은?

Amnesty International was formed in 1961 ① <u>to defend</u> human rights throughout the world. Created by a British lawyer, it now has more than 2.2 million members. The number of members working to help people who face unjust imprisonment ② <u>is</u> increasing. The main goal of Amnesty International is to assist those who ③ <u>have been punished</u> for their political beliefs. It also exposes human rights violations, encourages governments to change laws, and ④ <u>conducts</u> campaigns to educate the public about human rights. Amnesty International ⑤ <u>awarded</u> the Nobel Peace Prize in 1977 for "having contributed to securing the ground for freedom, for justice, and thereby also for peace in the world." [기출 응용]

*Amnesty International: 국제사면위원회(정치범, 사상범의 석방 운동을 주도하는 국제 인권 단체)

3 다음 밑줄 친 부분 중 어법상 틀린 것을 두 개 찾아 기호를 쓰고 바르게 고치시오.

Colton, a city in California, is currently ⓐ <u>involved</u> in a series of legal battles over how much ⓑ <u>they</u> should be prepared to pay to save an endangered fly: the Delhi Sands Flower-loving Fly, a rather pretty insect that takes nectar from local flowers. This tiny creature has the distinction of being the first fly which ⓒ <u>was declared</u> an endangered species in the U.S. Shortly after this fly ⓓ <u>was listed</u> as an endangered species, construction of a hospital parking lot was stopped. The hospital ⓔ <u>has planned</u> to construct its parking lot over seven acres of occupied fly habitat, but that suddenly became illegal. The hospital then had to spend $4 million redrawing its plans and ⓕ <u>moving</u> its parking lot 250 feet. [기출 응용]

4 다음 밑줄 친 부분 중 어법상 틀린 것을 모두 찾아 기호를 쓰고 바르게 고치시오.

While humans ⓐ <u>may have shifted</u> from signs to speech long ago, Stokoe and Armstrong don't consider sign language primitive. In fact, they believe just the opposite. "My work in sign language," says Stokoe, "is to let people know that the hearing-impaired are just as bright and able to handle abstract thought as ⓑ <u>heard</u> people, given equal education. Prejudice against them because they don't speak any languages ⓒ <u>leading</u> to all sorts of bad judgments about the hearing-impaired. ⓓ <u>Recognizing</u> the fact that we all probably owe a great deal to the era when language began in a gestural state might change some of that. The first language may have been a language not of voices but of signs." [기출 응용]

1 다음 글의 밑줄 친 부분 중, 어법상 **틀린** 것은?

When we evolved from living on all fours to ① <u>living</u> on just two, life changed dramatically. We run marathons, walk shopping malls that are as large as entire counties, and ② <u>spend</u> summers hiking a trail that reaches from Georgia to Maine. No matter where we're walking, our feet endure some serious abuse. With twenty-six bones in our feet, we were made to move. But our feet don't have the natural shock absorbers other parts of the body ③ <u>have</u>. To better protect them, always ④ <u>wearing</u> well-cushioned walking or running shoes when you are on your feet for lengthy periods of time. Running shoes are usually a good option because they're well cushioned in the back of the shoe, where your heel strikes the ground first and ⑤ <u>absorbs</u> most of your body's weight.

2
도전

다음 글의 밑줄 친 부분 중, 어법상 **틀린** 것은?

Everybody knows that ① <u>during</u> the winter months, we often tend to feel "blue." Some doctors say ② <u>that</u> this seasonal sad feeling is caused by a lack of sunlight. It is certainly true that people kept indoors all day suffer from "cabin fever," a miserable feeling that you get when you are shut up inside for too long. But people who live in concrete buildings and walk paved streets all their lives ③ <u>lack</u> a lot more than sun. They may lose their link to fresh air, green scenery, and all the happiness ④ <u>what</u> nature has to offer. Of course, activities like gardening, mountain climbing, hiking, or just eating outside can help. But in the long run, we need to do something about our cities. We need to make spaces ⑤ <u>where</u> we can get the light, fresh air, and contact with nature that we were born for. [기출 응용]

3 다음 밑줄 친 부분 중 어법상 틀린 것을 두 개 찾아 기호를 쓰고 바르게 고치시오.

Psychologist James Cutting claims that the originals of the most reproduced works of impressionism today ⓐ are thought to have been bought by five or six wealthy and influential collectors in the late 19th century. The preferences of these men gave prestige to certain works, which made the works more likely to be hung in galleries and ⓑ print in anthologies. The popularity of these works grew over the years, and ⓒ they gained the interest of many people. ⓓ The more people liked them, the more they appeared in books, on posters and in big exhibitions. Meanwhile, academics and critics created sophisticated justifications for their excellence. After all, it's not just average citizens who tend to rate ⓔ that they see often more highly. As contemporary artists like Warhol and Damien Hirst have grasped, critical acclaim is deeply related to publicity.

4 다음 밑줄 친 부분 중 어법상 틀린 것을 모두 찾아 기호를 쓰고 바르게 고치시오.

If people in a relationship spend time together, the relationship will ⓐ strengthen. Likewise, the enterprise will prosper if the partners agree on basic goals, plans, strategies, and the like. When common goals, plans, and strategies are discussed, clarified, and worked toward, they provide a binding force that can compensate for many of the ⓑ predictably differences between people. For example, if a couple has the goal of saving a set amount of money to put toward a down payment on a house, they will work toward ⓒ it, plan together, and arrive at specific steps to achieve that goal, thereby drawing themselves closer together. On the other hand, if one member wants continually to buy as many creature comforts as possible, or eat often at expensive restaurants, while ⓓ another wants to save for a rainy day, the couple will be torn apart by these differences.

*creature comforts: 삶을 안락하게 하는 것들(좋은 음식·기구·현대적 장비 등)

MEMO

MEMO

POWER UP

파워업
듣기 모의고사

40회

1
최신 경향 반영 실전 대비
듣기 모의고사 40회 수록

2
총 4명의 남/여 원어민
성우 참여로 살아있는
회화체 표현

3
MP3 QR CODE
PLAYER 무료 제공

4
핵심표현 DICTATION과
다양한 부가서비스 제공

쎄듀북닷컴(www.cedubook.com)에서 부가 자료를 무료로 다운로드할 수 있습니다.

쎄듀

쎄듀런

1 구문 · 판매 1위 '천일문' 콘텐츠를 활용하여 정확하고 다양한 구문 학습

주어진 기호를 사용하여 문장 구조를 분석하고, 해석을 완성하시오.

It will not do to dismiss magic as nonsensical, information available affects what is rational, …

주어진 기호를 사용하여 문장 구조를 분석하고, 해석을 완성하시오.

주어진 기호를 사용하여 문장 구조를 분석하시오.

Anne Frank's diary was found hidden in the upper floor where the Frank family hid.

우리말과 일치하도록 주어진 단어를 올바르게 배열하시오.

(끊어읽기) (해석하기) (문장 구조 분석) (해설·해석 제공) (단어 스크램블링) (영작하기)

2 문법·서술형 · 쎄듀의 모든 문법 문항을 활용하여 내신까지 해결하는 정교한 문법 유형 제공

다음 밑줄 친 부분이 어법상 알맞지 않은 세 개를 골라 바르게 고치시오.

ⓐ A man has special experiences during his military serive.

ⓑ Such an experience can be frightening as well as excited for

ⓒ Although she had an umbrella, she got very wet.

다음 밑줄 친 부분이 어법상 올바르면 O로, 어색하면 X를 선택하고 …

주어진 우리말과 일치하도록 괄호 안의 단어를 활용하여 <조건>에 맞게 영작하시오.

다음 문장에서 틀린 곳을 하나 찾아 밑줄을 긋고 이를 바르게 고치시오.

(객관식과 주관식의 결합) (문법 포인트별 학습) (보기를 활용한 집합 문항) (내신대비 서술형) (어법+서술형 문제)

3 어휘 · 초·중·고·공무원까지 방대한 어휘량을 제공하며 오프라인 TEST 인쇄도 가능

major

주어진 단어의 올바른 뜻을 고르시오.

electronic

빈칸에 들어갈 알맞은 단어를 고르시오.

단어와 뜻이 일치하도록 연결하시오.

(영단어 카드 학습) (단어 ↔ 뜻 유형) (예문 활용 유형) (단어 매칭 게임)

4 선생님 보유 문항 이용

TEST 부정사의 3가지 용법

☕ cafe.naver.com/cedulearnteacher

쎄듀런 학습 정보가 궁금하다면?

쎄듀런 Cafe

· 쎄듀런 사용법 안내 & 학습법 공유
· 공지 및 문의사항 QA
· 할인 쿠폰 증정 등 이벤트 진행

(Online Test) (OMR Test)

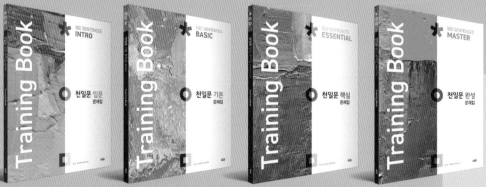

고등 *All New* 어휘끝

WORD COMPLETE

접사와 어근으로 의미를 파악하는 어휘 추론력부터
다양한 문맥 속에서 정확한 뜻을 파악하는 진정한 어휘력까지!

고교기본 → 수능

고교기본	수능
중3 ~ 고1 1,200개 표제 어휘	**고2 ~ 고3 1,800개 표제 어휘**
본격적인 수능 학습은 이르지만 빠른 고교 기본 어휘 학습이 필요할 때	본격적인 수능 대비를 위해 좀 더 난이도 있는 어휘 학습이 필요할 때!

쎄듀런 Mobile & PC
고등 어휘끝
일부 유형 온라인 학습권 무료 증정
고등 어휘끝 고교기본 · 수능 전체 어휘 수록

7가지 유형 반복 학습으로
내 머릿속에 영원히 저장!

[무료] 영단어 카드 학습

explode
🔊
图 폭발하다, 폭파시키다; 폭증하다
The number of smartphone users has **exploded** in recent years.
스마트폰 사용자 수가 최근 몇 년 간 폭증해 왔다.
↺ 뒷 감추기 / Tone offer
NEXT
Enter Key

[유료] 영단어 고르기

4/25
주어진 뜻의 올바른 단어를 고르시오.
[동] 폭발하다, 폭파시키다; 폭증하다
1. explode
2. blend

[유료] 뜻 고르기

8/25
주어진 단어의 올바른 뜻을 고르시오.
explode
1. 굽히다, 구부러지다
2. 묻다, 매장하다

[유료] 예문 빈칸 고르기

4/25
빈칸에 들어갈 알맞은 단어를 고르시오.
The boat _____ to the bottom of the sea.
→ 그 보트는 바다 밑까지 가라앉았다.
1. approach
2. explode
3. bury

[유료] 예문 빈칸 쓰기

1/25
다음 우리말에 알맞은 영어를 쓰시오.
아이처럼 행동하지 마라.
Don't _____ like a child.
⟲ 힌트보기 / ⌫ 지우기

[유료] 영단어 쓰기

2/25
다음 우리말에 알맞은 영어를 쓰시오.
围 다가가다, 다가오다, 접근하다 (= come near) 围 접근(법)
_ _ _ _ _ _ _ _
⟲ 힌트보기 / ⌫ 지우기

[무료] 단어 매칭 게임

⏱ 제한 시간 03:38
단어와 뜻이 일치하도록 연결하세요.
정답 단어 : 2개 / 출제 단어 : 25개

| ...ay | bang | 围 환불하다 围 환불(금) | explode | 다가가 하다(: |
| ...und | 围 꽉으로 잡다, 함정에 빠르 리다; (위험한 장소, 궁지에) 가두다 围 덫, 함정 | peel | 围 콩 소리가 나게 닫다, 콩 소리가 나게 치다 围 (쾅 하는) 소리 | (종이나...) |

쎄듀캠퍼스 유료 상품 구매 시 7가지 전 유형으로 학습하실 수 있습니다. (50% 할인쿠폰 제공)

쎄듀북닷컴(www.cedubook.com)에서 부가 자료를 무료로 다운로드할 수 있습니다.

쎄듀

쎄듀 초·중등 커리큘럼

	예비초	초1	초2	초3	초4	초5	초6
구문		천일문 365 일력 |초1-3| 교육부 지정 초등 필수 영어 문장		초등코치 천일문 SENTENCE 1001개 통문장 암기로 완성하는 초등 영어의 기초			
문법					초등코치 천일문 GRAMMAR 1001개 예문으로 배우는 초등 영문법		
			왓츠 Grammar		Start (초등 기초 영문법) / Plus (초등 영문법 마무리)		
독해				왓츠 리딩 70 / 80 / 90 / 100 A / B 쉽고 재미있게 완성되는 영어 독해력			
어휘				초등코치 천일문 VOCA&STORY 1001개의 초등 필수 어휘와 짧은 스토리			
		패턴으로 말하는 초등 필수 영단어 1 / 2		문장 패턴으로 완성하는 초등 필수 영단어			
ELT	Oh! My PHONICS 1 / 2 / 3 / 4		유·초등학생을 위한 첫 영어 파닉스				
		Oh! My SPEAKING 1 / 2 / 3 / 4 / 5 / 6 핵심 문장 패턴으로 더욱 쉬운 영어 말하기					
		Oh! My GRAMMAR 1 / 2 / 3 쓰기로 완성하는 첫 초등 영문법					

	예비중	중1	중2	중3
구문		천일문 STARTER 1 / 2		중등 필수 구문 & 문법 총정리
문법		천일문 GRAMMAR LEVEL 1 / 2 / 3		예문 중심 문법 기본서
		GRAMMAR Q Starter 1, 2 / Intermediate 1, 2 / Advanced 1, 2		학기별 문법 기본서
		잘 풀리는 영문법 1 / 2 / 3		문제 중심 문법 적용서
		GRAMMAR PIC 1 / 2 / 3 / 4		이해가 쉬운 도식화된 문법서
			1센치 영문법	1권으로 핵심 문법 정리
문법+어법		첫단추 BASIC 문법·어법편 1 / 2		문법·어법의 기초
문법+쓰기		EGU 영단어&품사 / 문장 형식 / 동사 써먹기 / 문법 써먹기 / 구문 써먹기		서술형 기초 세우기와 문법 다지기
				올쌤 1 기본 문장 PATTERN 내신 서술형 기본 문장 학습
쓰기		거침없이 Writing LEVEL 1 / 2 / 3		중등 교과서 내신 기출 서술형
		중학 영어 쓰작 1 / 2 / 3		중등 교과서 패턴 드릴 서술형
어휘		신간 천일문 VOCA 중등 스타트/필수/마스터		2800개 중등 3개년 필수 어휘
		어휘끝 중학 필수편	중학 필수어휘 1000개	어휘끝 중학 마스터편 고난도 중학어휘 +고등기초 어휘 1000개
독해		신간 ReadingGraphy LEVEL 1 / 2 / 3 / 4		중등 필수 구문까지 잡는 흥미로운 소재 독해
		Reading Relay Starter 1, 2 / Challenger 1, 2 / Master 1, 2		타교과 연계 배경 지식 독해
		READING Q Starter 1, 2 / Intermediate 1, 2 / Advanced 1, 2		예측/추론/요약 사고력 독해
독해전략			리딩 플랫폼 1 / 2 / 3	논픽션 지문 독해
독해유형			Reading 16 LEVEL 1 / 2 / 3	수능 유형 맛보기 + 내신 대비
		첫단추 BASIC 독해편 1 / 2		수능 유형 독해입문
듣기	Listening Q 유형편 / 1 / 2 / 3			유형별 듣기 전략 및 실전 대비
		쎄듀 빠르게 중학영어듣기 모의고사 1 / 2 / 3		교육청 듣기평가 대비